THE CLAY-FOOTED SUPERHEROES

LATIN FOR THE NEW MILLENNIUM
Series Information

LEVEL ONE
Student Text (2008)
Student Workbook (2008)
Teacher's Manual (2008)
Teacher's Manual for Student Workbook (2008)

ANCILLARIES
From Romulus to Romulus Augustulus:
Roman History for the New Millennium (2008)
The Original Dysfunctional Family:
Basic Classical Mythology for the New Millennium (2008)

LEVEL TWO
Student Text (2009)
Student Workbook (2009)
Teacher's Manual (2009)
Teacher's Manual for Student Workbook (2009)

ANCILLARIES
The Clay-footed SuperHeroes:
Mythology Tales for the New Millennium (2009)
From Rome to Reformation:
Early European History for the New Millennium (2009)

ELECTRONIC RESOURCES
www.lnm.bolchazy.com
Quia Question Bank
Latin-only Villa in Teen Second Life™
Carpe Praedam
Electronic Vocabulary Flashcards

THE CLAY-FOOTED SUPERHEROES

SUPERHEROES

 MYTHOLOGY *FOR THE* NEW
TALES MILLENNIUM

By Rose Williams

Bolchazy-Carducci Publishers, Inc.
Mundelein, Illinois USA

Editor: Donald E. Sprague

Cover Design & Typography: Adam Phillip Velez

Cover Illustration: Heracles on the Façade of the Hofburg Palace in Vienna, Austria © 2009 Jupiter Images Corp.

The Clay-footed SuperHeroes
Mythology Tales for the New Millennium

Rose Williams

Bolchazy-Carducci Publishers, Inc.
1570 Baskin Road
Mundelein, Illinois 60060
www.bolchazy.com

Printed in the United States of America
2009
by United Graphics

ISBN 978-0-86516-719-3

Library of Congress Cataloging-in-Publication Data

Williams, Rose.
 The clay-footed superheroes : mythology tales for the new millennium /
by Rose Williams.
    p. cm.
 Includes bibliographical references.
 ISBN 978-0-86516-719-3 (pbk. : alk. paper) 1. Heroes--Mythology--Greece. 2.
Heroes--Mythology--Rome. 3. Mythology, Greek. 4. Mythology, Roman. I. Title.
 BL795.H46W55 2009
 398.20938'02--dc22

                                                                    2009027580

TABLE OF CONTENTS

PREFACE

Greece gave the western world its first widely-known superheroes. From Heracles who brained his music master with a lyre to Theseus who in a forgetful moment left the princess who had saved his life on a deserted island, they fell a few furlongs short of the standard of perfection. Yet they were handsome and resourceful, they faced death without flinching, and they overcame almost insurmountable odds. It is not surprising that their stories have held the unflagging interest of a hundred generations and have played a key role in literature and art through those generations.

Terms that might be unfamiliar to the reader are emphasized in bold-face type upon their first appearance. The notes section at the back of the book provides an explanation for the terms.

The Clay-footed SuperHeroes was designed to serve as an ancillary and quick reference book for any group studying literature or the ancient world. It is a good resource for those using the Bolchazy-Carducci textbook *Latin for the New Millennium, Level 2* and coordinates as follows.

COORDINATION WITH CHAPTERS IN *LATIN FOR THE NEW MILLENNIUM*

I.   Sons of Gods and Men

       Heracles, Perseus, Theseus, Jason (LNM 2, Review 1)

II. Dysfunctional Dynasties

       House of Atreus, House of Labdacus (LNM 2, Review 4)

III. Heroes, Gods, and Wooden Quadrupeds

       The Trojan War (LNM 2, Review 2)

IV. Going Back to Greece

       The Atreides and Odysseus (LNM 2, Review 3)

V.   Starting Over

       Aeneas and the Beginning of Rome (LNM 2, Review 5)

NB: There are multiple versions of these myths. Furthermore, commentators from Euhemerus in the fourth century BCE to Robert Graves in the twentieth century CE have interpreted them as reflections of actual events. The versions I have followed can be found in the Ancient Sources listed at the end of this book.

INTRODUCTION

Hero is a greatly overused word. In today's society it applies to anyone who does something for someone else without expectation of reward, and this definition is basically acceptable. The word is also loosely used as a synonym for idol to indicate anyone who is well-known or admired for any reason, from singing rock music to looking nice in a bathing suit. This use of the word does a disservice to the richness of its history in western culture.

The classical Greco-Roman hero was a mortal who underwent one or more ordeals, often on a mission or quest performed under the eyes of hostile powers and likely to end in his death, which he hoped to meet in a way that would earn him *kleos*, or immortal glory. The story of Heracles underlines this point. His name has been translated "Glory of Hera"— the goddess who spent quite a bit of time trying to destroy him.

Humans, all of whom also live in the constant shadow of death, are drawn to personalities who can face this ultimate disaster without cowering, as that attitude gives a certain freedom to live fully. As Aeneas tells his men while the Greeks are burning Troy down around them, "The one safety is to stop hoping for safety" (*Aeneid* 2.354).

The average human, who sometimes feels that the whole universe, or at least a significant part of it, is capable of destroying him, can identify with several aspects of the classical hero: he was often beset by antagonistic powers from birth or even before birth, he had questionable aspects in his family background, which was of prime importance in the ancient world, he gave or risked his life for others, and he often "came to rest" in an unknown grave.

Once the hero had achieved *kleos*, after death he often became a cult figure who was given festivals and sometimes even temples, and expected in return for these honors to protect his worshippers in death as he had done in life, and to provide prosperity. Sometimes this prosperity came in the form of fertility of plants and animals; sometimes as inspiration for the worshippers in war, allowing them, like Aeneas, to achieve safety by ceasing to look for it.

I: SONS OF GODS AND MEN

PERSEUS
THE QUEST FOR THE GORGON'S HEAD

Most Greek heroes in childhood were beset by some power dead set on seeing that they never grew up. Perseus' situation began even earlier. His prospective grandfather, King Acrisius of the Greek city of Argos, did not want his daughter to have any children, and took great precautions to see that she never met any men.

This anti-descendant attitude of Acrisius seems a bit strange, but it was the result of his asking the **Delphic Oracle** of Apollo the god of truth whether he would have any male heirs. Apollo could never lie, but his oracle often made up for this possible handicap by skirting around the suppliant's question and flooring him with a bit of truth guaranteed to give him high blood pressure, if not outright apoplexy. Acrisius was informed that he would be killed by his daughter's child. With that stubborn, and totally useless, shortsightedness so typical of characters in ancient myth, Acrisius tried to forestall the oracle by imprisoning his daughter Danae in an underground bronze house with only a small opening for light and air. Here he was sure no man could reach her. No man did. But that did not solve Acrisius' problem.

Zeus, grandson of Heaven and Earth and youngest child of **Cronus** and Rhea, had become Lord of the Sky and General Superintendent of the Universe upon dethroning his father. From his lofty position he had an excellent view of the Earth and a special appreciation for its loveliest inhabitants, an appreciation which made Hera, his wife and queen, furious. She was not only Queen of the Gods, but also the protectress of marriage, which in her case proved to need a great deal of protecting.

Acrisius' precautions helped not at all; there was absolutely no future in trying to conceal lovely girls from Zeus. Eluding both Acrisius' precautions and Hera's watchful eye, Zeus showed the ingenuity he always used when engaged in mischief and visited Danae in a shower of golden rain. Soon she gave birth to a baby boy whom she named Perseus.

Upon discovering that, in spite of his best efforts, he had become a grandfather, Acrisius faced a dilemma which would come upon many other ancient characters. The **Erinyes**, or Furies, visited those who killed relatives. Since these immortal female avengers had snakes for hair and eyes that wept tears of blood, people were reluctant to encourage them to make an appearance. Therefore he put Danae and her son Perseus in a wooden chest and floated them out to sea, smugly reflecting that he had done no violence and that what happened to them next was no concern of his. Zeus, who always, if he happened to remember, kept an eye on his offspring, asked his brother Poseidon the sea god to calm the waves.

The chest washed ashore on the island of Seriphos, and the seafarers were taken in by Dictys, the brother of King Polydectes. After some years Polydectes fell in love with Danae, who was still beautiful though Perseus was now a young man. Perseus was very protective of his mother, and Polydectes decided to get rid of him. The king announced his approaching marriage, and invited all to the wedding, knowing that they would bring gifts and that Perseus, who had no source of income, would have nothing to bring. When the humiliated young man faced the king and his court, with the rashness and anger so typical of the young, he announced that he would bring as a gift anything that Polydectes might want. Polydectes, with the nastiest smile imaginable, said he wanted the head of Medusa. Perseus immediately swore that he would not return without it. Polydectes took great interest in the part about not coming back, as this was the outcome he expected. Medusa was one of the three Gorgons, monstrous females with snakes on their heads instead of hair and with bodies covered with impenetrable golden scales. To make matters worse, two of them were immortal, and they all looked alike. Not that this fact had up to this point made a great deal of difference, as everyone who looked at them turned to stone.

Perseus wandered around for quite a while trying to find the Gorgons' island, which was not on the map, before Hermes the messenger god and Athena goddess of wisdom came to his aid. No one knows why they did this; perhaps Zeus had taken a somewhat tardy interest in his son and encouraged the intervention of these half-siblings on Perseus' behalf. Hermes appeared, complete with winged sandals and winged hat, and gave Perseus some valuable though circuitous information. He said that Perseus, to put it mildly, needed some special equipment to deal with the Gorgons. He went on to say that this equipment was in the possession of the nymphs of the North, and that Perseus must go to the Graiae to find out how to get to these nymphs. These three Gray Women lived in the land of twilight, and possessed only one eye among them, which they took turns using. They were extremely stingy with information, so Perseus was instructed to hide until one nymph started to hand the eye to the next; then he had to leap out, grab it, and refuse to give it back until they told him how to find the nymphs of the North. Evidently this was a test for Perseus, as Hermes, messenger of Zeus, knew very well where the nymphs were. He promised to guide Perseus to the Graiae, and also to lend him a sword which could not be bent or broken by the Gorgon's scales. Athena turned up at this point and gave Perseus her shield to carry, so that he could look into the polished metal and see the reflection of the Gorgon and cut off her head without looking at her.

After a long and shadowy journey Hermes and Perseus arrived at the twilight land. Perseus was somewhat taken aback at the sight of the Graiae, as they looked like swans except for having human heads and arms with hands beneath their wings. Still, he snatched the eye as instructed, and was told that the nymphs he sought lived with the Hyperboreans, a blessed race who lived at the back of the North Wind feasting and celebrating. Hermes led him there, and the nymphs stopped dancing long enough to give him three gifts: winged sandals, a bag which was always the right size for whatever was put in it, and a cap which made the wearer invisible. Perseus, now fully armed, was guided by Hermes to the island of the Gorgons.

By great good fortune (or the contrivance of some god) the Gorgons were all sleeping when Perseus arrived. Hermes and Athena were beside Perseus, pointing out which Gorgon was the mortal Medusa. Looking in the shield and guided by Athena, Perseus cut off Medusa's head and dropped it in the bag. Then man and gods departed quickly, as the other two Gorgons awakened with a start.

Hermes and Athena went about their divine business, and Perseus started the long flight home. As he flew over Ethiopia, he saw a strange sight—a maiden chained to a rock. He discovered later, when he had the leisure to ask, that she was Andromeda, the daughter of King Cepheus and an extremely foolish queen named Cassiopeia, who had boasted that she was more beautiful than the daughters of Nereus the sea god.

Perseus triumphantly displays the head of the much-feared Medusa.

Whether or not this was true was completely beside the point. Such *hubris* always drew the wrath of the gods, who sent a sea serpent to devour Cepheus' people and announced they would withdraw it only if his daughter Andromeda were offered to the serpent. Perseus, still showing that impetuosity typical of youth in general and mythological figures in particular, fell in love with her on the spot, waited beside her until the serpent came, and relieved said beast of his head. He then flew back to the palace and asked Andromeda's parents for her hand in marriage, which they gladly gave him.

When he arrived with his bride on Seriphos he found that all was far from well. Dictys and Danae were hiding from Polydectes, who was still furious with Danae for refusing to go ahead with the marriage. Perseus left Andromeda with them and went straight to the palace where Polydectes and his henchmen were feasting. He strode in noisily and, when everyone looked up, whipped Medusa's head out of the bag and considerably increased the island's supply of statues.

Having made Dictys King of Seriphos, Perseus took Danae and Andromeda and went back to Argos to see if they could make peace with Acrisius, but the king had gone on a journey, and no one knew where. Then Perseus went to Larissa, where he had heard of a great athletic contest. He entered the javelin throw, and as anyone who has read many Greek myths could have foretold, it swerved into the crowd and killed an elderly spectator, who just happened to be King Acrisius.

After he learned what he had done, Perseus, not wanting his grandfather's throne under these circumstances, exchanged cities with his cousin Megapenthes, who became king of Argos while Perseus became king of Tiryns, and according to the ancient Greeks, founded Mycenae. Later Tiryns went to war with Argos, and Perseus was killed. He left many sons, and after various contretemps among them Sthenelus succeeded his father as king of Tiryns, Electryon received Mycenae, and Perses ruled Ethiopia and became ancestor of the emperors of Persia.

Perseus was gone, but, in the manner of classical heroes, far from forgotten. Pausanius mentions the shrine to Perseus that stood on the left-hand side of the road from Mycenae to Argos, and also a sacred fountain at Mycenae called *Persea*.

HERACLES
THE QUEST FOR ABSOLUTION

Perseus had left entirely too many offspring. Electryon King of Mycenae was accidentally killed by Amphitryon, son of another **Perseid**. Amphitryon was exiled for this, and fled with his cousin Alcmene to his maternal uncle Creon, King of Thebes, who cleansed him of his blood guilt. Amphitryon married the beautiful Alcmene, but he was not alone in admiring her. Zeus, still observing precautions, came to Alcmene in the guise of her husband, and she bore two sons: the mortal Iphicles to

Amphitryon and Heracles to Zeus. This evidently worked splendidly until Zeus, in a moment of hare-brained euphoria, boasted that a son soon to be born to him would be High King of the mighty house of Perseus. This little bit of thoughtlessness provided Heracles one feature necessary to a hero—the antagonism of a great power. Hera (who never seemed to miss these little tidbits) set out to destroy him.

Hera had hindered Alcmene's delivery so that another queen would bear her son first, making that child heir to the high kingship. She then turned her divine attention to shortening Heracles' life. She sent two giant serpents into the cradle of Heracles and Iphicles. Hearing the screams of Iphicles, Alcmene ran into the nursery to find Heracles laughing and holding a strangled snake in each hand. In no way discouraged, Hera set out to torment Heracles with the same thorough nastiness she would show in dealing with the Trojans after the Trojan War.

After he flew into a boyish rage and brained his music master with a lute, Heracles was relegated by thoughtful mentors to the outdoors, where he killed the Thespian lion which had been devastating the woods of Cithaeron. Ever after he wore a lion skin, either this one or perhaps the skin of the Nemean lion, who was soon to be another of his victims.

He was given the princess Megara in marriage as a reward for defeating the Minyans and ridding the Thebans of a pesky **tribute** paid to that people. This loving couple had three sons, and the sight of Heracles enjoying all that bliss was more that Hera could bear. She drove him mad, and he killed his wife and children. Then, with her typical thoroughness, Hera restored his sanity so that he could understand what he had done. As the trembling Thebans filled him in on the details, he vowed to kill himself. Before he could rush forth to do so, his friend and kinsman Theseus of Athens clasped his bloodstained hands to share in his guilt and begged him to come to Athens, be strong, and leave death come when it would. Heracles went, but he could not share the philosophical reasoning of the Athenians, who insisted that he could not be guilty of a murder he had not known he was committing. Heracles was a man of great strength and feeling, but philosophical reasoning was quite beyond him. His guilt drove him to the Delphic Oracle, which told him, with a clarity unusual for it, that he must be purified, and sent him to his cousin Eurystheus King of Mycenae for instructions as to what he must do.

Eurystheus, who wanted no competition from a fellow Perseid who was much braver and stronger than he himself was, devised a really fiendish set of tasks known as the Labors of Heracles. In this charming exercise he was helped, of course, by Hera, who had yet to finish punishing Heracles, not only for existing in the first place, but also for being Zeus' favorite son.

Each of the labors was chosen with the amiable intention of cutting short Heracles' career, and great was the dismay of Eurystheus and Hera when the hero accomplished each one.

The first labor was to kill the Nemean lion, whose hide could be pierced by no weapon. Heracles solved this difficulty by choking it to death. When he appeared in Mycenae with the huge carcass on his shoulder, Eurystheus turned a ghastly pale color and ordered him henceforth to deliver his trophies outside the city.

Second Heracles killed the nine-headed Hydra, which grew two more heads when he chopped off one. He solved this problem by searing the necks as he chopped off the heads, a tactic which worked well until he came to the last head, which was immortal. This he cut off and buried under a rock and the Hydra died at last. (How an immortal head grew on a mortal body was one of those little conundrums with which Greek mythology never troubled itself.)

There is some disagreement about the exact order of the next labors, but they were these: he had to capture alive both a stag with golden horns and hooves and the great Erymantian boar. To Eurystheus' dismay he brought these back alive to show this taskmaster.

After that he cleaned the stables of Augeas, who had not attended to the matter for years, by diverting a river through them; killed the Stymphalian birds who were plaguing a city; and went on two more animal hunts, one for the savage bull belonging to King Minos of Crete and one for the man-eating horses of Diomedes, both of whom he brought back alive.

The ninth labor involved a change of pace—he was to bring back the girdle of Hippolyta, the queen of the Amazons, those fierce women warriors who inhabited a fortified island. She kindly gave him the girdle, but Hera, who did not like the way the labors were turning out, exhorted the Amazons to fight him and he killed the queen and fought off the Amazons.

For the tenth labor Heracles had to bring back the cattle of Geryon, a three-bodied monster who lived on a western island. Heracles paused on the way to set up the pillars of Heracles at the western end of the Mediterranean, on each side of what is now called the Strait of Gibraltar, then killed Geryon and brought back the cattle.

As this was not working out the way Eurystheus and Hera had planned, the tasks grew even harder, though that is hard to imagine. Number Eleven was to bring back the Golden Apples of the Hesperides. Nobody but Atlas, the Titan who had been holding the vault of heaven on his shoulders ever since he had been on the wrong side of the War of the Gods, could tell him where the Hesperides, who were his daughters, actually lived. Heracles set out to find Atlas, pausing on the way to free Prometheus, who had angered Zeus by giving fire to humankind and had consequently been chained to a rock for eons, while an eagle of Zeus ate his liver every day and the immortal liver grew back every night. Heracles slew the bird and freed Prometheus. When he arrived at his destination, Atlas said that, if Heracles would hold the sky for a while, he would go and get the golden apples. When Atlas returned, he told Heracles that he would take the apples to Mycenae while Heracles continued to hold the world. Heracles was no Athenian philosopher, but he could see that Atlas was less than enthusiastic about taking his burden back. Heracles was in no position to deal with him while supporting the sky, so he had to use whatever brainpower he could muster. He agreed to hold the world, but asked Atlas to hold the sky while he got a pad for his shoulders. As Atlas was no great intellectual himself, he reassumed the burden, and Heracles broke all speed records for the trip to Mycenae.

Labor Number Twelve, both Eurystheus and Hera knew, had to be the *piece de resistance*. Heracles was ordered to bring up from Hades the giant three-headed dog Cerberus, who guarded the entrance. Heracles knew better than to try to storm the realm of his uncle Hades, god of the dead. His first stop was at Eleusis for two reasons. First, he wanted to be purified for the death of some **centaurs** he had happened to finish off in an odd moment. Second, he wanted to become an initiate into the **Eleusinian Mysteries**, which precaution men engaged in hazardous tasks often took in order to gain the protection of the powerful Eleusinian gods. After this, he journeyed down to the Underworld, pausing to free Theseus, who had helped with a feckless plot to steal Persephone, Hades' queen, and was consequently imprisoned in the Chair of Forgetfulness. Arriving at last, Heracles politely asked Hades' permission to borrow Cerberus. Hades agreed, provided that Heracles overcame his dog without the use of weapons. Heracles subdued the beast with his bare hands, took him to Mycenae, and placed him at the foot of the throne of Eurystheus, who could only gasp out, "Take him back." Heracles restored Hades' pet, and his labors were at an end.

A medieval rendering of Hades shows the three-headed Cerberus in the center of the Underworld assembly. Visiting the Underworld and returning safely constituted a very significant heroic achievement.

Heracles had many more adventures and killed many more people, some unintentionally. His last wife was Deianira, whom he loved devotedly. The two set forth on a journey from Calydon, and met the centaur Nessus, who helped them cross a river. The centaur tried to carry off Deianira, so of course Heracles killed him, with an arrow this time. This was an unfortunate choice, because it gave Nessus time before he died to instruct Deianira to gather a vial of his blood, which he said was a potent love charm which she could use if she ever thought she was losing the love of Heracles. Years later Heracles sent back a band of captive maidens, among whom was a beautiful young princess, Iole. Some busybody told Deianira that Heracles was madly in love with the girl, and she hastened to anoint a beautiful soft robe with the blood of Nessus and give it to her husband. Heracles put on the robe and instantly felt fire in all his limbs. Deianira killed herself when she saw what she had done, but Heracles was too strong to die this way. He had a great funeral pyre made. He gave his bow and arrow to his faithful follower Philoctetes and lay down upon the pyre, where he was immediately surrounded by flames and taken up to Mount Olympus to dwell with the gods. There he was reconciled to Hera and given one more wife, Hera's daughter Hebe, goddess of youth.

Many ancient temples and shrines memorialized Heracles, or Hercules, his Roman counterpart. The Greeks celebrated a festival called the Herakleia.

THESEUS
THE QUEST FOR DELIVERANCE

Aegeus King of Athens had had two wives but no heir, and he was worried. Being a good Greek, he went to consult the Delphic Oracle, which gave him an answer less appalling than the one Acrisius had received, but also much vaguer: "Don't loosen the wineskin until you have reached the height of Athens." While taking an overnight rest in the town of Troezen, he told his host King Pittheus, who was known for his wisdom, about the oracle's words. Pittheus, understanding only too well what the oracle meant, gave Aegeus a great deal of very potent wine and then introduced him to a lovely maiden, Aethra. In the morning Aegeus learned that Aethra was the daughter of Pittheus, and he put two and two together concerning the recent events. He showed Aethra a great rock under which he placed a sword and a pair of sandals. He said that if their child was a boy, he should take these things from beneath the rock and come secretly to Athens. He feared that his nephews, who wanted the throne, would make short work of his heir.

Pittheus and Aethra reared the child, a boy whom they named Theseus, concealing his heritage and spreading the rumor that he was the son of Poseidon, the god of the sea. When he was old enough, Aethra showed Theseus the rock and told him the story, and day by day he gained strength and tested himself against it. At last he was strong enough to lift it and obtain the sword and sandals underneath. Then she and her father offered him a ship to go to Athens. Theseus, already aware of the exploits of his kinsman Heracles, chose to be brave and go overland. Though the sea had its dangers, the land route was infested with hostile kings and robbers. He made the hazardous land route considerably less hazardous by killing the robbers which infested it, and all Greece rang with the praise of the unknown young man.

Medea the witch in the meantime had fled to Athens and the protection of King Aegeus when she had made Corinth too hot to hold her by arranging the death of a princess with a robe like the one given to Heracles. Knowing through her sorcery who Theseus was, she told Aegeus that such a popular young man would take the kingdom from him.

The palace at Knossos with its multiple storeys, winding corridors, hundreds of rooms, and natural light shafts readily gave rise to the myth of King Minos' labyrinth.

She persuaded Aegeus to invite the young man to a banquet and poison him there. While she was holding the poisoned wine for Aegeus, Theseus drew a sword Aegeus knew only too well, and Aegeus snatched the cup from Medea and threw it away. Medea fled to Asia, and Aegeus welcomed his son and proclaimed him heir to the throne.

Soon after these stirring events the great sorrow of Athens reared its ugly head. Some years before, the powerful king of Crete, Minos, had sent his only son Androgeos on a state visit to Athens, and King Aegeus had been dumb enough to let the young man go on a hunt to kill a dangerous bull. The bull had killed the boy, and a furious King Minos had stormed Athens and said that he would raze it to the ground unless the Athenians sent him a tribute of seven maidens and seven youths every nine years. His revenge was to put these young people into the Labyrinth, the great maze which Daedalus the inventor had built for him to contain the Minotaur. This winsome creature was half man and half bull, the offspring of Queen Pasiphae and a marvelous bull which Poseidon had given to King Minos and which Minos should have had the good sense to sacrifice to Poseidon instead of keeping for himself. Poseidon had caused the queen to fall in love with the bull, and the Minotaur was the result of this lamentable affair. For some inscrutable reason it ate the people it found in the Labyrinth, and this was to be the fate of the young Athenians. Theseus offered to be one of the sacrificial victims, telling his father that he would kill the beast and, on returning to Athens, would change the black sail that the ship of doom always carried to a white one.

King Minos, on receiving the young sacrifices, made an arrogant mistake. He paraded the victims through the streets on their way to the Labyrinth, and his daughter Ariadne fell in love with Theseus as he passed. She immediately cajoled Daedalus into telling her how to escape from his Labyrinth, and smuggled this information, plus the necessary equipment, to Theseus. The process was amazingly simple: he merely carried a ball of string and unrolled it as he went through the maze, keeping the other young Athenians behind him and instructing them to keep watch for the Minotaur in case it might suddenly appear from one of the endless passages. By luck he found the Minotaur asleep and killed it, some say with a sword, some say with his bare hands. (This sounds a bit incredible, but sacrificial bulls were often struck at the base of the brain with a mallet to kill them; perhaps Theseus, strengthened by his exploits, was able to strike such a blow with his fists.) Gathering up his ball of string, he hastily rewound it, and, taking the other Athenian youths and Ariadne, fled in his ship which some thoughtless soul had left handy.

On the voyage home Theseus did two things that the ancient authors labor greatly to explain. He put in at the island of Naxos, and left Ariadne behind there. Then he sailed home to Athens without changing the black sails to white as he had promised his father he would do.

A forlorn Ariadne awakens after napping on Naxos only to find herself abandoned by Theseus whom she loved dearly.

All accounts agree that Theseus sailed away from Naxos and left Ariadne there. Now this does not seem very heroic, and the ancient writings give widely varying explanations. Apollodorus says that the god Dionysus had fallen in love with Ariadne, and carried her off. He then says that Theseus was heartbroken, and forgot to change the sails. Another version says that Ariadne was set ashore because she was ill, and the ship was carried out to sea. The Roman poet Catullus, who had his own reasons for doubting the faithfulness of lovers, said that she fell asleep and in a moment of absentmindedness Theseus sailed away without her. He goes on to say that she cursed him so that the same thoughtlessness led to his forgetting to change the sails. However that may have been, Aegeus, seeing the ship returning with black sails, leapt into the sea which would ever after be known as the Aegean.

Theseus became an excellent king, credited with the unification of the territory of Attica under his Athenian rule and protecting the downtrodden, from the bloodstained Heracles to the disgraced king Oedipus to the losers in the war of the Seven against Thebes when they wanted the right to bury their dead.

He was still an adventurer, though, in spite of these kingly qualities, taking part in the Calydonian Boar Hunt and carrying off an Amazon, Antiope or Hippolyta. She bore him a son, Hippolytus, but the Amazons came to rescue her, invading Athens itself but finally being defeated before they could destroy it.

Pirithous, King of the Lapithae, was as harebrained as he was brave. Having heard of the valor of Theseus, he decided to test it by carrying off some of the cattle of Theseus. When Theseus came full-speed after him, Pirithous was overcome with admiration, meeting Theseus with outstretched hand and offering to submit to any penalty for his rash action. Theseus asked only for the friendship of this charming rogue, and they were fast friends ever after. This was lucky for Pirithous, for when he married Hippodamia, a group of Centaurs, those half-man, half-horse creatures came to the feast, where they proceeded to get drunk and tried to carry off the women. Theseus defended the bride and led the Lapithae in driving the Centaurs out of their country.

The rescued bride was not long-lived, however, and Pirithous with his usual foolhardiness decided that he wanted Persephone, Queen of Hades, for his next. Theseus loyally accompanied him to the Underworld, where they both wound up the in Chairs of Forgetfulness.

Heracles rescued Theseus, but Hades would not allow the rescue of Pirithous, who was the chief culprit, and evidently he is still there. Meanwhile Theseus' current wife Phaedra, the sister of the problematic Ariadne, had fallen in love with her stepson Hippolytus. Some say this was because he had worshipped only Artemis the hunting goddess and scorned Aphrodite, the goddess of love, who had her own way of avenging such slights. Hippolytus turned in disgust from Phaedra, who killed herself and left a letter for Theseus saying that she had done this because Hippolytus had attacked her. Theseus called upon Poseidon to curse his son, and banished Hippolytus. As Hippolytus drove his chariot along the seacoast, a sea monster frightened his horses and he fell mortally wounded from the chariot. As he was carried dying to Theseus, Artemis (who could have bestirred herself a bit earlier to help her devotee) told Theseus the truth.

Perhaps Theseus may have been too long away; perhaps the death of Hippolytus had sickened the people. One way or another, Theseus had lost his firm hold on the Athenian people. He retired in disgust to the court of King Lycomedes of Scyros, where the king for obscure reasons cast him into the sea. Sometime later Kimon returned his ashes to Athens, and the Thesia, or festival of Theseus, was instituted. His remains were interred and his grave became a sanctuary for people in peril, in keeping with the best traditions of his life. Fragments of Philochorus indicate that there were at least four shrines or temples to Theseus at Athens.

JASON
THE QUEST FOR BIRTHRIGHT

Jason, who came from Thessaly in Northern Greece, was in ancient eyes not exactly an equal of the Perseids, who not only had at least tenuous claims to divine ancestry but also were associated with Attica and its environs. However, his lineage was hardly to be despised. He was descended from Hellen, the patriarch of all Greeks or Hellenes. His father was King Aeson of Iolcos and his mother Alcimede was descended from the Boeotian King Minyas. Unfortunately his grandmother, Aeson's mother Tyro, had had a liaison with Poseidon which produced twins, one of whom was his frightful uncle Pelias. As gods were notoriously protective of their offspring, this could have proved fatal for Aeson's branch of the family when Pelias developed royal ambitions. However, Pelias and his twin sought revenge on Sidero, whom Aeson's father King Cretheus had married in a careless moment and who had mistreated their mother Tyro. They pursued her into the temple of Hera, where suppliants were supposed to receive sanctuary, and killed her on the altar there, thus earning the hatred of Hera. The goddess deeply resented this insult and would thereafter give aid in any plans made against Pelias.

Jason was an infant when Pelias made his move, overthrowing Aeson and killing Aeson's descendants. Alcimede secretly sent her son Jason off to the wise centaur Chiron for education. Meanwhile Pelias ruled uneasily, and often consulted the oracles, one of which cryptically told him to beware of a man wearing only one shoe.

Grown to manhood, Jason came to the city of Iolcos during a great festival in honor of Poseidon. On the journey he met an old woman, who asked his help in crossing the river Anauros; while helping her he lost, of course, one of his sandals. Readers acquainted with Greek mythology will not be surprised to learn that the old woman was Hera in disguise, and that Pelias turned a ghastly white when he heard of the fine young man who had entered his city wearing only one shoe.

Pelias, confronted by Jason on the question of his right to the kingdom, admitted that Jason was the rightful king, but reminded him that his great-uncle Athamus had had twin children, Phrixus and Helle, who had been scheduled for sacrifice due to the machinations of their stepmother and saved by a flying golden ram which Zeus (or in some stories Poseidon) sent to whisk them away. The princess Helle had fallen into the water later called the Hellespont, but Phrixus had been kindly received by King Aetes. He had sacrificed to the gods the golden ram, which became the constellation Aries. He then had given its golden fleece to King Aeetes, who had hung it in a tree guarded by a dragon that slept neither by night nor day. Now, Pelias said, the Golden Fleece must be brought home so that the spirit of Phrixus could return to the land of his ancestors. "Do this," said Pelias, "and I swear by Zeus that I will give you the throne of our kingdom." The young man eagerly took the quest, and Pelias settled back with the smug feeling that he had seen the last of his troublesome nephew.

Jason prayed to Hera and to Pallas Athena for aid, promising sacrifices such as the divinities loved. Athena hurried to consult Argos of Thespiae, who some said was a son of Phrixus come from Colchis. Whether or not this was true, he was certainly a shipbuilder, and that was what Jason needed. Hera meanwhile was proclaiming throughout her cities Jason's quest and its promise of glory for heroes.

Everybody who was anybody answered the call. Argus built a mighty ship from the talking wood which Athena provided. This strong and chatty ship, which sometimes gave Jason very good advice, was christened the *Argo*, and thus the sailors were known as Argonauts. Among these great adventurers were Argus; Bellerephon who had ridden the winged horse Pegasus; Castor and Polydeuces, known as the Dioscuri or sons of Zeus; Heracles, who was derailed by the loss of Hylas before Colchis was reached; Zetes and Calais, who as twin sons of the North Wind Boreas could fly; Orpheus the great musician; Peleus the father of Achilles; and many others. Some ancients say Theseus went along; others say he was on the Chair of Forgetfulness down in Hades and therefore missed the ship.

On their sea journey the Argonauts experienced many adventures, including a stay on Lemnos, the Island of Women, and a visit with the prophet Phineas, who repaid them for ridding him of **Harpies** by telling them the secret of Symplegades, or the Clashing Rocks, which stood on each side of a narrow passage and slammed together to the destruction of anything passing between them. He told them to release a dove and time the resulting crash. The dove escaped, losing only a few tail feathers, and the Argonauts rowed for dear life in the time it took the rocks to reposition themselves for another onslaught. The ship, like the dove, lost only a bit of tail ornament, the *Argo* triumphantly sailed on, and the Symplegades were so embarrassed that they never moved again.

Aeetes received them kindly in Colchis, promising to give them the fleece if Jason would do him a small favor, i.e., yoke two fire-breathing bulls, plow a field with them, sow dragon's teeth, and then kill the crop of warriors which would promptly spring up. While Jason was achieving these simple tasks, the king's daughter Medea, who luckily was a witch, fell in love with Jason. When her father tried to go back on his word, she put the dragon who guarded the fleece to sleep, and she and Jason, complete with Golden Fleece, fled to the *Argo* and the heroes set sail. When her father tried to follow them, she cut her little brother Absyrtus, whom she had brought along as insurance, into pieces so that her father would have to pause to gather him up and then give him a proper burial. After an adventurous trip home involving the twin dangers Scylla and Charybdis, they arrived in Iolcos only to learn that Pelias had no intention of honoring his word. Medea tricked his daughters into killing him.

At this point the stories vary. Some say the Iolcians were so incensed over the manner of the death of Pelias that they drove Jason and Medea out; others say that he ruled. However that may have been, he decided, after ten years and two sons with Medea, to marry the daughter of the king of Corinth. Medea sent the bride-to-be a poisoned robe, which burst into flame when donned, killed her own two sons, and fled to Athens in a dragon-drawn chariot sent by her grandfather the sun god Helios. Jason, on a visit to the decaying *Argo*, was killed when a beam fell on him.

II: DYSFUNCTIONAL DYNASTIES

THE HOUSE OF LABDACUS

Labdacus was King of Thebes and grandson of Thebe's founder, Cadmus. He is important to mythology chiefly because he is the grandfather of Oedipus **Tyrannos**, the most tragic of all Greek mythological figures. Oedipus was another of those children who were unwanted—even before birth. King Laius, son of Labdacus, consulted the Delphic Oracle, which handed down one of those hair-raising prophecies. He was told that if he had a son with his wife Jocasta, the child would kill his father. Laius, understandably horrified, decided upon a chaste relationship with Jocasta, which he was unable to maintain. When their son was born, the child became another of those Greek heroes somebody powerful did not want to grow up: Laius ordered Jocasta to destroy the child. Most stories say that she passed child and instructions on to a herdsman, who pierced the child's feet and tied them with thongs, evidently to make more certain that the baby exposed on the mountainside would die. This gave the baby his name, Oedipus, the "Swollen-Footed." He was found by another herdsman, who gave him to his own master, King Polybus of Corinth. Polybius reared the child as his own son.

When grown, Oedipus consulted the Delphic Oracle, which ignored his original question, but calmly informed him that he would kill his father and marry his mother. Horrified, Oedipus left Corinth, vowing never to see his parents again. His travels, of course, took him to Thebes. En route he fell into a dispute with an irascible old man about the right of way at a crossroad, and killed him in the heat of argument. Having read this far about the heroes of Greek mythology, one can readily surmise that this irascible old man was Laius, King of Thebes.

Continuing his journey, Oedipus found his way barred by the Sphinx, a lion-like creature with a woman's head, who asked everyone on the road to Thebes a riddle and devoured them if they could not answer. "What," she demanded of Oedipus, "walks on four feet in the morning, two at noon, and three in the evening?" Most people waylaid by the

Sphinx were too frightened to use what wits they had, but Oedipus was both brave and unhappy, and fear meant little to him. After a moment's thought he said, "Man. He crawls in the morning of his life, walks upright in its noonday, and uses a cane in its evening." The Sphinx on hearing the correct answer killed herself, and the people of Thebes were too happy in their liberation to wonder why. They welcomed the victorious young stranger into their city, and of course, he married their queen.

This reincarnation of the Sphinx in the gardens of the Belvedere Palace in Vienna, Austria, presents a formidable image. Note that the Greek sphinx is female while the famous Sphinx of Giza, Egypt, is male.

Years later, when Oedipus and Jocasta had four grown children—two sons, Polyneices and Eteocles, and two daughters, Antigone and Ismene—a plague struck Thebes. Oedipus sent Creon, Jocasta's brother, to the Oracle at Delphi, which promptly stated that the murderer of Laius must be found and punished by death or exile. Oedipus, as was his habit in confronting oracle or prophet, insistently questioned the blind prophet Tiresias, who warned him not to try to find the killer. Oedipus persisted, and finally Tiresias informed him that he was himself the killer he was seeking, and that he did not even know who his parents were. A messenger arrived to say that King Polybius of Corinth was dead, and Oedipus panicked at the idea that he might marry his mother. The messenger, seeking to reassure him, informed him that he was adopted, and once again he went seeking the truth. His quest led to the old herdsman who knew the history of Polybius' adopted son. A stunned Oedipus put the facts together. Jocasta, horrified, ran into the palace. Oedipus followed Jocasta and found that she had hanged herself. He took a brooch from her gown, blinded himself, and went forth as a bleeding beggar, accompanied by his daughters. His sons scorned him and he laid a curse on them that would soon and thoroughly be fulfilled. At Colonus, a village near Athens which was sacred to the Erinyes, Theseus of Athens offered him refuge and there he is said to have died.

Meanwhile Eteocles and Polyneices, sons of Oedipus, agreed to share the kingdom, each ruling for one year. Eteocles ruled first, and refused to relinquish the throne. Polyneices went to Argos for help, and came against his home city Thebes with forces led by seven great warriors, one for each of the seven Theban gates. In the battle the two brothers killed each other, and Creon, the brother of Queen Jocasta, took the throne. He then ruled that, as Polyneices was a traitor to his home city, he and those who fought with him should not be buried. Antigone buried her brother anyway, and faced the wrath of Creon. Theseus, called on by various relatives of the attacking warriors, showed up with the Athenian army to force the burial of all the dead, but by this time all Creon's family had either killed each other or committed suicide, leaving him alone. In later years he was killed and supplanted by Lycus.

This horrendous story, which still attracts much attention and analysis, troubled the ancient writers to such an extent that it was constantly rewritten; thus its details are many and varied. It appears that Oedipus, who acted in innocence, received no justice from the gods. The playwrights, attempting to deal with this, accuse Oedipus of *hubris* in forcing the issue at every turn and say he should have known better. Sophocles in *Oedipus Tyrannos* even makes him say that forcing the gods against their will is beyond human power, while he continues to do so.

THE HOUSE OF ATREUS

The house of Atreus got off to a bad start with Tantalus, son of Zeus and a nymph. Tantalus was favored by the gods, but he was the poster child for that Greek besetting sin, *hubris*. He invited the gods to a banquet and served his son Pelops as the main course, intending to make cannibals of them without their knowledge. The gods of course immediately realized his perfidy, all except Demeter, who was absentminded through grief for her lost daughter Persephone and ate some of the boy's shoulder. The gods restored Pelops to life, giving him an ivory shoulder, and sent Tantalus down to Hades to stand forever in water up to his neck while starving for a drink. Pelops became King of Elis, won the maiden Hippodamia in a chariot race, and had two sons, Atreus and Thyestes. It seems he had another son, Chrysippus, child of a liaison with a nymph, and that Atreus, Thyestes, and Hippodamia murdered this child and fled to Mycenae. Mycenae was ruled by the king who gave Heracles all those labors—the Perseid Eurystheus, who had married Pelops' sister Nicippe. After the death of Heracles, Eurystheus, still not satisfied, went to war against Heracles' descendants, whom he considered rivals for his throne. He was killed in combat. Atreus and Thyestes both wanted Mycenae's throne, but Atreus triumphed. Thyestes avenged himself by seducing Atreus' wife Aerope. When Atreus found out, he killed Thyestes' two little sons and served them to their father. Not being as wise as the gods, Thyestes only found out about this after dinner. Neither he nor the gods ever forgot, however, and Atreus and his children would pay a price for this hideous deed.

In time Atreus had two sons, Agamemnon and Menelaus, but Thyestes also had a son, Aegisthus, who killed Atreus and placed his father Thyestes on the throne. Agamemnon and Menelaus then fled to Sparta, where they were received kindly by King Tyndareus. Agamemnon married Tyndareus' daughter Clytemnestra, and with his help drove out Thyestes and Aegisthus to become the king of Mycenae.

Tyndareus was head of a rather peculiar family, thanks to Zeus who had fallen in love with his wife Leda and visited her in the form of a swan. She had given birth to two children of Tyndareus, her son Castor and her daughter Clytemnestra, and two children of Zeus, her son Polydeuces and her daughter Helen. Clytemnestra was beautiful and strong-willed, but Helen was the most beautiful woman on earth, and she had been wreaking havoc among men since her early childhood. A regular platoon of kings, nobles, and upstarts had descended on her supposed father King Tyndareus demanding her hand in marriage. No doubt he had already decided that Menelaus would make a fine son-in-law, but before he committed himself, Tyndareus, who was no fool, made all the hopefuls swear to support Helen's husband in the quarrels that were extremely likely to arise concerning her. Every man, modestly expecting to be the winner, happily swore the oath. (A few minutes later most of them were just swearing.) Of course admiration of her charms was not likely to be limited to Greeks, and the time would come when she would be the cause of the Trojan War, the most stupendous conflict the classical world had ever seen.

III: HEROES, GODS, AND WOODEN QUADRUPEDS

THE TROJAN WAR

On the west coast of Asia Minor stood a great city, Troy, which was ruled by a descendant of Zeus, King Priam. Priam had been warned by the **seer** Aesacus and Apollo's Sibyl Herophile that his infant son Paris would be the destruction of his native city. As the father of fifty sons, Priam had had a few to spare, so he had followed the usual tradition of having the dangerous babe left on a mountainside, in this case Mount Ida. As we have seen, babes abandoned on mountainsides were extremely likely to be rescued by wandering herdsmen. Paris fared well on Mount Ida, playing the pipes and charming the nymphs, one of whom was his beloved, Oenone, until one of those little contretemps which did so much to liven up life among the gods on Mount Olympus turned nasty.

Eris, goddess of Discord, was not invited to the marriage feast of King Peleus and the sea nymph Thetis, because everywhere she went she started a fight. She resented the slight, and decided to avenge herself by her favorite activity—starting a fight. Well aware of the high temper and acquisitive nature of goddesses, she tossed on the banquet table a golden apple inscribed "For the Most Beautiful." It was immediately claimed by Aphrodite, who had the best right to it, by Hera, who as Queen of Heaven thought she had a right to all goodies, and by Athena, who as goddess of wisdom should have known better. Zeus was far too well acquainted with the female sex to have anything to do with the resulting squabble. He sent them down to Mount Ida, recommending Paris as an excellent judge of beauty.

Somewhat startled at the sudden overpopulation of goddesses in his small glade, Paris balanced the golden apple in his hand as he listened in awe to the details of the beauty contest. The deities wasted no time with the bathing suit and talent competitions: they got right down to the bribes. Hera promised Paris power over Europe and Asia; Athena, victory against the Greeks, and Aphrodite; with a slight smirk, offered him the most beautiful woman in the world. Needless to say, Aphrodite readily received the apple.

Now we know that the most beautiful woman in the world was already married to the powerful King Menelaus of Sparta. Aphrodite knew this too, and also knew that Helen's powerful husband, because of the oath Tyndareus had demanded, could exploit the oath of a plethora of even more powerful kings and warriors. The goddess, however, had never been one to consider any of the possible consequences of her playful little actions. She instructed Paris, for openers, to scrap the shepherding and go down to Troy and present himself in the role of Lost Heir.

When Paris appeared he was welcomed with open arms (evidently Priam had a short memory for oracular prophecies) and the aforementioned disastrous results set in with unusual ferocity. Sent on a diplomatic mission to Menelaus King of Sparta, Paris returned not with the king's trade agreement but with his wife. The Greek leaders, considering the effort they had spent in trying to marry the beautiful Spartan queen themselves, foamed at the mouth to think that an intrusive outsider had made off with the prize from under Menelaus' royal nose. While they were grumbling about how much better care they would have taken of Helen if her bumbling supposed father had chosen one of them as her husband, Agamemnon and Menelaus sent out the call to arms. Greek leaders recollected that pesky oath they had taken and collected a thousand ships in order to sail to Asia Minor and show the Trojans what they thought of such pilfering.

Among the former suitors two important heroes did not heed the call to rally but preferred to hold out. One was Odysseus, son of Laertes, one of the Argonauts, and king of the island of Ithaca. Odysseus had married Penelope, King Tyndareus' niece. He had a lovely wife, a small son, and a flourishing kingdom; he was already becoming known for an unusual mixture of common sense and inventive cleverness. Because of the first, he had no interest in leaving all his possessions to go running off to Troy after the queen Menelaus had been stupid enough to lose. Because of the second, when the messengers came for him, they found him plowing worthless ground and sowing it with salt instead of seed. Unfortunately for him he was not the only clever Greek. One of the messengers, Palamedes, set Odysseus' infant son Telemachus before the plow; Odysseus quickly turned to save his child, and everyone knew he was not crazy.

The second holdout was the great warrior Achilles. (As we know, the trouble that led to the Trojan War began at the wedding of Achilles' parents, the sea nymph Thetis and King Peleus of the Myrmidons. The fact that Achilles is already known as a hero by the time the war begins is one of those little discrepancies which never bother Greek mythologists.) Achilles' mother Thetis had never been enamored of the idea of her son as a warrior, but she had done her best to make him invulnerable by dipping him in the river Styx when he was a baby. She had held him by one heel, however, and only in that spot could he be wounded. When the Trojan War was being planned she became really upset, because she knew that if he went to Troy he would die there. She persuaded him to go to the court of Lycomedes, King of Skyros, and hide there among the women. While there, although he dressed in women's clothes during the day, he managed with the cooperation willing or otherwise of Lycomedes' daughter Deidamia to father a perfectly appalling son, who would become the brutal warrior Neoptolemus or Pyrrhus.

Odysseus decided that if he had to go, Achilles might as well join him. He went to Lycomedes' court disguised as a peddler. In the women's quarters everyone gathered around the jewelry and silks, except for one tall young lady who was fingering the spears. Odysseus, having located Achilles, encountered little trouble persuading him to join the adventure.

The great Greek fleet had assembled at the port of Aulis, but the winds they needed to sail east to Asia Minor did not blow because Artemis, goddess of hunting, was angry. Some thoughtless Greek had killed one of her sacred animals. She demanded as a sacrifice the eldest daughter of Agamemnon, who had been chosen leader of the Greek army, to regain her favor. The horrified Agamemnon eventually gave in, and sent a deceitful message to his wife Clytemnestra requesting her to send Iphigenia to Aulis so that she might be married to the great hero Achilles before the fleet sailed. When Clytemnestra complied, she met Achilles, and promptly congratulated him on his approaching nuptials, of which no one had yet informed him. The two of them confronted Agamemnon, with Achilles saying he would defend the girl brought to slaughter by the use of his name. When Iphigenia saw what was happening, she volunteered to be sacrificed to avert a war in the Greek camp. Iphigenia died, and the fleet sailed for Troy. Clytemnestra went home to spend the ten years of the Trojan War planning a suitable homecoming for Agamemnon.

A grieving Clytemnestra mourns the imminent sacrifice of her beloved daughter Iphigenia. In Euripides' plays, Iphigenia is rescued by the goddess Artemis who makes her a priestess of her temple.

For nine years the war raged on the plain below the great walls of Troy with no discernible advantage on either side. The Greeks led by Achilles were great on offense, but the Trojans led by Hector, eldest son of King Priam, were equally strong on defense. Each of these heroes was a startlingly handsome specimen of young manhood, even in a poetic tradition where all males were expected to be handsome and all females beautiful. Each was the best warrior in a community of great warriors. Each had the athletic strength and skill that ancient warfare demanded combined with heroic valor and the relentlessness to kill without mercy or pity. Strong, bold, and seemingly disdainful of wounds and death, they were inspirations to their people. Achilles and Hector differed greatly, however, as is shown by their reasons for joining the battle. Achilles came because of his desire for *kleos,*or glory, while Hector defended his home and family from attack. For Hector and his cousin Prince Aeneas, family love and loyalty were central. This is not true of Achilles, who was solely driven by his passionate desire to achieve *kleos* In the *Iliad* (9.410–16) Achilles told Odysseus, Ajax, and Phoenix that his mother had told him that he could choose between *kleos* with an early death or a long life which would be uneventful. He had chosen *kleos*, and all his acts were directed toward this end. He would have stood off the entire Greek army at Aulis rather than have his name sullied by the deceit which brought Iphigenia to the sacrificial altar.

Hector as well as Achilles knew that he fought under the shadow of certain death, but the *kleos* he achieved by the greatness of his deeds did not weigh greatly on him. In the *Iliad* (6.446–47) he told his wife Andromache that he knew well that Troy would fall. He also told her (6.486–89) that no man could send him down to Death before the destined time, and that a man must fight for his home and his loves until that time arrives. Then, with a tender word for her and their little son Astyanax, he went back into the fight.

Homer's epic concentrates on a sudden shift at the beginning of the tenth year of the war. Agamemnon had carried off a maiden, Chryseis, who was the daughter of Apollo's priest Chryses. Being refused when he asked for his daughter's return, Chryses prayed to Apollo, and the golden arrows of the sun slew more Greeks than the Trojans did. Everybody knew what the trouble was, and saw that the war would soon be lost, but only Achilles was brave enough to confront Agamemnon. All the Greek chieftains ranged themselves with Achilles, and Agamemnon had to yield. When Chryseis was gone, however, Agamemnon took as a replacement the maiden Briseis, who was Achilles' prize of war. This proved a grave mistake, because it brought out some facets of Achilles' character that, to put it mildly, could throw a wrench into the engine of progress. Achilles' vaunts or boasts while standing with his foot on the chest of brave men he had just killed and telling how great they were before he slew them are unattractive, but typical of Homeric epic. However, he also possessed inordinate pride, an easily outraged sense of fair play, and what some would consider a childish stubbornness. When his prize was taken from him, after all he had done was tell Agamemnon the truth, he promptly sat down in his tent and refused to fight, wanting to show the Greeks that they could not succeed without him.

Agamemnon and two great Greek warriors, Ajax and Diomedes, led the forces out against the Trojans to little avail. The Greeks without Achilles were not equal to the Trojans led by Hector and his cousin and brother-in-law, Aeneas, who was the son of Anchises, a prince in Troy's sister city Dardania, and the goddess Aphrodite. The gods by now, heedless of Zeus' admonition to stay out of the war, were ranged on one side or the other. Hera and Athena, still smarting over that apple business, joined the side of the Greeks, while Apollo, Aphrodite the mother of Aeneas, and Ares joined the Trojan side. Diomedes wounded Aeneas, then struck Aphrodite's arm when she came to assist Aeneas. Aeneas was then rescued by Apollo, because he had a destiny beyond this war. Artemis healed Aeneas' wound, and he promptly went back into the fight. Diomedes came face to face with Hector, but fell back when he saw Ares fighting beside him. Athena then wounded Ares, and he fled. Hector's brother Helenus, a seer, told Hector to take a little time out and go back to the city to instruct his mother Queen Hecuba to give Athena an offering and thereby try to win her over to the Trojan side.

The Greek warriors depicted beside the impregnable walls of Troy.

As the war raged on, things continued to go very badly for the Greeks. The Trojans with Hector and Aeneas in the lead were driving the Greeks back to the ships. Agamemnon was thinking about giving up and sailing home. Nestor, the oldest and wisest of the Greek chieftains, told Agamemnon it was all his own fault for having angered Achilles. Agamemnon agreed, but all his apologies and gifts, Briseis included, did not sway Achilles. He refused to fight, but his friend Patroclus, seeing the Greeks making a desperate stand at the ships, borrowed Achilles' armor and went into the fray. The Trojans drew back a little, but Hector, who had been longing to come to blows with Achilles, killed Patroclus and took the magnificent armor of Achilles for his own. The death of Patroclus and the loss of his armor immediately changed Achilles' mind. Rearmed by his helpful mother Thetis, who had persuaded Hephaestus, the great blacksmith god, to make new armor for her son, Achilles roared out into battle, seeking revenge. The Trojans fled before him, and Hector stood alone to face him before the walls of Troy. With Athena at his side, Achilles came after Hector, killed him, and, crazed by the loss of his dear friend Patroclus and no doubt feeling guilty and yet again showing petulant childishness, mercilessly dragged Hector's body around the walls of Troy before his parents' eyes. The gods were displeased with this maltreatment of the dead; after all, Hector had only done to Patroclus what Achilles had done to countless warriors. Zeus sent old Priam to Achilles to ask for the return of Hector's body, and sympathy overcame Achilles when Priam asked him to think of his own father, just as easily as childish rage had motivated him previously. Priam's request was granted, and a nine days' truce was declared for the funeral of Hector. Achilles knew he would not long survive Hector and while sitting out of the war he contemplated his fate, a choice concerning living a long life without fame or a short but glorious one. It did, however, seem rather unfair that he was killed by an arrow shot into his heel by Paris, who had done little in the war even though he had provoked it and had demonstrated the least heroism of all the Trojan princes.

The seemingly endless war wore on. The Greeks tried everything they could think of or that the prophets could suggest, from bringing back Heracles' bow and arrows from the deserted island where they had left his heir Philoctetes to stealing the Palladium, a sacred image of Athena, from Troy. The arrows of Heracles killed Paris, but he was no great loss. The Palladium did not seem to help much, so Odysseus conceived the idea of building a giant wooden horse, hiding soldiers inside, and leaving it outside the city with one wily liar named Sinon primed with a tale to persuade the Trojans to take the horse into the city. The Greeks, except for this liar, sailed away and hid behind the nearby island Tenedos.

The next morning Trojans looking over the walls saw that on that badly trampled beach in front of the walls of Troy amidst the usual litter of garbage stood an immense wooden horse. The Greeks and Greek ships were nowhere to be seen. The Trojans trooped out of the city to take a little tour of the beach, and were soon divided into Optimists and Pessimists. The Optimists said that the Greeks had grown tired and gone home. The Pessimists muttered, "They're up to something." As to the wooden horse, opinions were again sharply divided. A Trojan saddled with the name of Thymoetes, grandfather of all naïve Optimists, howled, "Let's take it into the city and anchor it in the citadel." Capys and many other Trojans had the admirable good sense to wonder why an enemy who had brought a thousand ships over the sea and fought the Trojans for ten years should suddenly disappear and leave behind a farewell present. "Push it into the sea," some suggested. "Light a bonfire under it." "Cut a hole in it." While the Trojans debated and the Greeks inside the horse listening to these cheery suggestions trembled, a priest whom Vergil calls "burning Laocoon" came running down the beach. He was shouting that "Beware of Greeks bearing gifts"—a quote that many thousands of unoffending (well, mostly unoffending) students have had to memorize, often in Latin (*Aeneid* 2.44). He then threw a spear into the side of the horse. A rattle of metal inside resounded and some unwary Greek let out a groan.

As the Trojans were discussing the probable implications of those suspicious noises from the horse, a group of shepherds rushed to King Priam, proudly showing off a very sorry-looking prisoner. This dejected-looking individual was Sinon, the aforementioned liar left behind by the Greeks because he was second in that skill only to Odysseus (who would not do in this case, as it had been necessary for him to set an example and take a place in his wooden horse if he expected anyone else to do so, and the Trojans already knew that Odysseus was a champion liar). Sinon, who was adept at looking pitiful, peered at the Trojans surrounding him and trembled a little. He said in a dull, hopeless voice, "Gods, what is left for me? The Greeks hate me; now the Trojans will have my blood" (*Aeneid* 2.71–72). Odysseus was no slouch at this sympathy-grabbing game. He had primed Sinon with a lie sure to appeal to the Trojans. After the mess the Greeks had been making of Trojan ecology (and of quite a few Trojans) for ten years, anybody the Greeks hated looked pretty good to them. So they settled down and asked him for his story. They got a great one, all about Odysseus having done in Sinon's powerful protector Palamedes, who had destroyed Odysseus' alibi for skipping this trouble-some war, and then having devised a plan to kill Sinon himself. "But," he interrupted himself, "you don't want to hear all that. Just kill me, like the Greeks want you to" (*Aeneid* 2.101–102). Of course, the Trojans begged him to give them the details, so he said that Odysseus had announced that the gods needed a human sacrifice and then rigged the drawing of lots so that Sinon would be the "Burnt Offering of Choice." He claimed to have escaped into the woods just in time. He also mentioned in passing that the wooden horse was a "get-home-safely" gift for the goddess Athena, and had been deliberately made huge so that the Trojans could not take it into the city and gain the goddess' favor. As an afterthought Sinon added that the Greeks hoped the Trojans would destroy it and make the goddess flatten them in a fit of pique.

The Trojans were feeling as merry as any people would who were suddenly rid of a long dismal war, and their good feeling (unfortunately for them) overflowed. They freed Sinon, promised he could be a Trojan, and prepared to pull the horse into the city. They were spurred on to this disastrous deed by the god Poseidon, who, undeterred by the fact that he had helped to build Troy, was now set on its destruction. (Exactly what he had against the place is uncertain; some say he had never been paid for his construction labors, but the facts were never revealed—no one dares question a god bent on mischief.) Laocoon was acting as Poseidon's priest that day, and as he prepared to kill the sacrificial bull, Poseidon sent a pair of his biggest and nastiest sea serpents to finish off Laocoon and his sons

The Venetian painter Tiepolo presents a fanciful interpretation of the great ruse of the Greeks.

in a particularly memorable way. The people took this as a sign that Poseidon was annoyed with Laocoon, and that it had something to do with his attack on that oversized horse. They hastily tore a hole in the city wall and hauled in the wooden monstrosity.

Under cover of night, of course, the Greeks sneaked out of the horse and easily opened the city gates since the Trojans had let the watchmen share the victory orgy. Their compatriots sneaked back across the water to wreak havoc and wreck anything else they could find. They set fire to the houses and killed the Trojans as they ran out. (This policy raises grave questions about Greek sportsmanship, but it certainly was effective.) Achilles' son, "raging Pyrrhus," (*Aeneid* 2.529–30) broke into Priam's palace and killed Priam's youngest son right in front of the old king. When Priam threw a trembling spear at him, Pyrrhus caught the old man by the hair, dragged him to the altar sliding in his own son's blood, and slew him.

Only Aeneas among the most notable Trojan warriors escaped this catastrophe. He fought as long as he could find a living Trojan to fight with him; then his mother Aphrodite came to him and told him to go back and rescue his family from the burning city. All the gods knew that he had a destiny, as Poseidon had indicated in *Iliad* 20.300–304 when he said the gods must see to it that Aeneas did not fight Achilles, although he, like a good warrior hero, was very much wanting to do this, because his fate was to ensure that the line of **Dardanus** should not perish. Aphrodite lifted the veil from his mortal eyes so that he could see the gods themselves helping to destroy Troy. He made his difficult way back to his house, lifted his aged father Anchises onto his shoulders, took his little son Ascanius (also known as Iulus) by the hand, commanded his wife Creusa to follow them, and set off through the burning streets. He told any Trojan he met to spread the word: survivors should gather in the wood outside the town where stood a ruined temple of Demeter.

When morning broke the Greeks collected their loot and their captives, threw the two-year-old son of Hector off the city wall so that he could never avenge his father, and loaded their ships for the long voyage home. Trojans who had escaped stayed quiet in the woods, awaiting Aeneas' orders.

IV: GOING BACK TO GREECE

THE ATREIDES AND ODYSSEUS

Starting home with their loot-laden ships, the Greeks soon learned that the gods who had helped them destroy Troy had not given them license to behave as they pleased. They had offended the gods in many ways in Troy, especially by despoiling the temples and dragging away captives who had sought shelter there. Therefore, the greater Greek fleet was separated on the journey home, different fleets were blown by storms in many directions, and many Greeks were killed by storm and shipwreck. Most of those who survived suffered great hardship.

Menelaus' ships, carrying him, his army, and his recovered queen Helen, were blown to Pharos, an island near Egypt, where they were becalmed for several years until Menelaus captured Proteus, the Old Man of the Sea. This ancient and peculiar sea-god could answer any question, but was extremely reluctant to do so. As he had the power to change his shape at will, questioners had to hold on to him while he became various species of flora and fauna, usually dangerous ones. Menelaus and his men sneaked up on him and held on desperately. Finally Proteus tired and told them what sacrifices they should make to gain safe passage back to Lacedaemonia, or Sparta.

Menelaus' brother Agamemnon fared much worse. His journey home was short, but he might have been better off, and certainly longer-lived, if it had lasted longer. Agamemnon's wife Clytemnestra had spent the ten years of the war making spectacular plans for his homecoming with the able assistance of his cousin Aegisthus, still smarting over the wrongs done to his father Thyestes. Clytemnestra welcomed Agamemnon home with great ceremony and a show of thankfulness. He should have been suspicious that she showed no jealousy, and in fact no interest, in his bringing home with him the Trojan princess Cassandra. With typical **Atreid** *hubris*, he loftily accepted her welcome and swept into the palace, only to be confronted with Aegisthus and a battle-axe. Cassandra, who had been beloved by Apollo and given the gift of prophecy, had refused

Apollo's advances. He had then arranged matters so that she would always foretell the future, but no one would ever believe her. Now, after having endured ten years of a war whose disasters she had constantly foretold to no avail, she spoke hysterically of the black deeds, past, present, and future, of this house. She then announced Agamemnon's death and her own, paid as little heed to the people who tried to hold her back as others had always paid to her, and went in the palace to face her death.

The prophetess Cassandra receives guests who seek her prophecy but will fail to heed it. The phrase "Cassandra prophecy" is used to characterize advice that is ignored.

Odysseus the Cunning, King of Ithaca, suffered the longest of all the return voyages. His intellect in addition to his bravery had ultimately brought the Trojan War to a successful conclusion, but he shared the wrath which the gods felt against all Greeks for their behavior during the sack of Troy. After a disastrous visit to the Island of the Cicones and an even more disastrous one to the Land of the Lotus Eaters, where all of his men could easily have drowsed away the rest of their lives feasting on this pernicious plant, Odysseus put in at the land, identified by later poets as Sicily, where the Cyclopes lived. The unprepossessing giants, who had one eye located in the middle of their foreheads, were always formidable, but Odysseus and his men chanced into the cave of one named Polyphemus. He came home in no hospitable mood, and, after blocking the door of the cave with a huge stone, he ate a couple of Odysseus' men for supper. Odysseus, to put it mildly, did not like the way things were shaping up, so, as usual, he made a clever plan. After giving Polyphemus some very potent wine as a guest gift and telling him that his name was Nemo, or Nobody, he waited until the giant went to sleep. Then, with the enthusiastic help of his frightened men, he sharpened the end of the giant's club to a point, hardened the tip

ODYSSEUS' JOURNEY
BACK TO GREECE

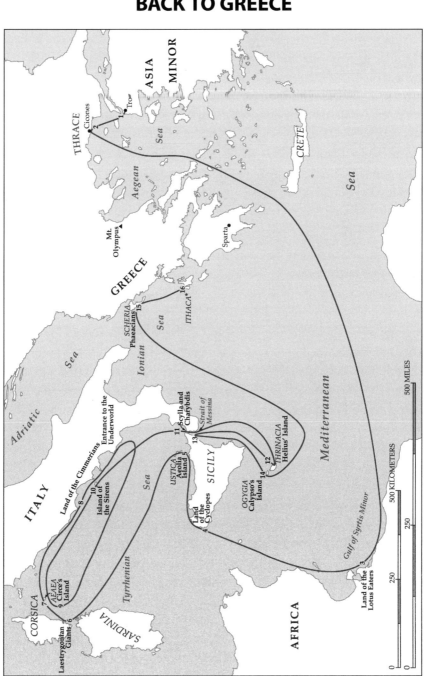

in the dying fire, and drove it into Polyphemus' eye. The giant bellowed, as might be expected, but when the other Cyclopes came to the door of his cave he said that "Nobody" had hurt him, so away they went.

Next morning Odysseus and his men clung to the fleece on the bellies of the sheep and were carried out of the cave. Blinded Polyphemus felt the back of each sheep, but did not have the wit to check the underneath. Safely back on the ship, Odysseus let loose one of those vaunts or boasts which are so common to Greek heroes, telling Polyphemus that it was Odysseus who had blinded him. Now the god Poseidon, who was already angry with Odysseus for giving him no sacrifice after he had sent those spectacular sea serpents to make the Trojans take the wooden horse into the city, was the father of Polyphemus, so this was not very wise of Odysseus. His act of *hubris* led to a number of watery and dangerous adventures.

After a visit to Aeolus, King of the Winds, which resulted in far too much air power, and an encounter with another race of man-eating giants, the Laestrygonians, Odysseus and his men landed at the island of Aeaea. If this name sounds like a scream, it should. This was the Isle of Circe, a beautiful and dangerous witch who whiled away her duller hours by turning any men who came her way into beasts—the four-footed kind. The poor fellows retained their reason but had inadequate voices to complain about their misfortunes. Only one of the scouting party Odysseus sent out on the island stayed outside Circe's palace, and he returned to Odysseus with the appalling news that the rest of the warriors were now swine. The king at once hurried off to the rescue, and was met on the way by the god Hermes, who told him to pick a nosegay of the herb moly, which would protect him from Circe's man-changing wine. She was impressed, and decided she was in love with him, but he insisted that she change his men back before there would be any romance. She agreed, and he spent a pleasant year on her island, after which she advised him to visit the prophet and seer Tiresias on his departure. There was one problem with this plan: Tiresias was in Hades, the world of the dead. Odysseus had to go to the gloomy land of the Cimmerians, on the frontier of the Land of the Dead, and there fill a trench with animal blood. Ghosts thirsty for this special drink would come, but Odysseus had to hold them all off until Tiresias came and drank. He gave Odysseus much good advice, including a warning to beware causing harm to the Golden Oxen of the Sun, a prohibition his men disregarded to their personal cost.

After hearing Tiresias, Odysseus permitted the other ghosts to drink, and heard his mother's account of her death, Agamemnon's complaints about being slaughtered by his wife Clytemnestra, and Achilles' bitter comments on Hades. "I had rather be the meanest slave on earth," Achilles said, "than lord among the dead" (*Odyssey* 11.488). Then so many ghosts thronged around the trench that Odysseus fled.

Circe had warned Odysseus of the Sirens and their enchanting song, so he blocked his men's ears with wax and escaped them, only to see ahead Scylla and Charybdis, who had merited special mention in the warnings he had received. Sailing round the toe of the Italian boot the traveler could see between Italy and the island of Sicily a narrow strait of water which was no place for ships. On one side of the narrow channel was the whirlpool Charybdis, sucking in the sea water and anything on it three times a day, then regurgitating its intake in little pieces. If a ship swerved to avoid Charybdis, it came within the reach of the fearsome inhabitant of the cave on the opposite shore. Said fearsome inhabitant was Scylla, an erstwhile beautiful maiden who had charmed a demigod that Circe the witch had wanted for herself. Circe had poured a little something extra into Scylla's bath water, which made dog's heads, serpents, and other unattractive features grow out of her body from the waist down. This had understandably blighted Scylla's outlook on life. As a result she had taken up residence in a cave on the shore opposite Charybdis, destroying everything and everybody she could reach. Circe advised staying closer to Scylla's side, as Charybdis could and would destroy the whole ship. Scylla snapped up six of Odysseus' men, but the rest escaped.

After this came the island inhabited by the Golden Oxen of the Sun. While Odysseus was taking a short nap, his men, heedless of all warnings, enjoyed a barbecue. Odysseus awoke and ordered them to sail away at once, but it was too late. The sun god, Helios or Hyperion in his old form or Apollo in a later one, told Zeus that he would leave the world in darkness if this deed were not punished. Zeus sent a thunderbolt which destroyed the ship and all the Greeks except Odysseus, who had had no part in the impious feast. He was wafted to the island of the nymph Calypso, who kept him as a captive lover for seven years. He wept by the seashore for his home, and at last Athena, who had been furious at all Greeks after the Trojan debacle, remembered her fondness for Odysseus, who had showed an intellectual power rare in Greek leaders. At her request Zeus sent Hermes to tell Calypso she must let Odysseus go home, and she helped him build a raft.

Now all this pro-Odysseus planning had been done while Poseidon, who was still furious about the blinding of his son Polyphemus, was off in Ethiopia feasting. Unfortunately Poseidon on his way back to Olympus spoiled the raft and immediately destroyed it. Athena chained all the

The Venetian painter Titian depicts Odysseus' arrival on the island of Calypso. Note his guardian Athena watching in the background.

winds except Boreas, the North Wind, who carried the water-logged Odysseus to the island of the Phaeacians. Then, while her exhausted mariner collapsed into a well-earned slumber, Athena arranged for Nausicaa, the daughter of Alcinous, king of the Phaeacians, to do the palace laundry with her handmaids near the spot where Odysseus had drifted ashore. Nausicaa discovered the interesting, seaweed-festooned stranger, and, having all that freshly-washed clothing at hand, provided the clothes which he sorely needed. She and the girls put on their best innocent faces and went back to town. After a while the stranger appeared and soon entertained her father's court with the story of his travels, and in turn they gave him a ship and many gifts for his homeward journey. Poseidon promptly sank the ship, but Athena spread a mist around Odysseus and his treasures, and he arrived at last in his own homeland. Athena appeared to him as a shepherd lad, and he promptly delighted her with a long tale about who he was and where he was going that contained not a word of truth. Laughing, she revealed herself. She told him, however, that all was far from well in his kingdom. They hid his gifts in a cave, and she turned him into a withered old man and sent him to the hut of an old swineherd, Eumaeus, to wait while she fetched his son Telemachus. Eager to search for his father or find out what happened to him, Telemachus had courageously taken on the challenge of the sea and traveled first to King Nestor and at the time of his dad's arrival home was enjoying hospitality at the palace of Menelaus. Much to his relief, Telemachus' identity as Odysseus' son was affirmed by Helen (formerly of Troy) who upon seeing the young guest at once announced that he very much resembled his famous father.

Telemachus was one of several royal offspring who had grown up during the long Trojan War and its aftermath and found themselves in difficulties. The assassination of Agamemnon had created quite a dilemma for Prince Orestes, son of Agamemnon and Clytemnestra. His sister Electra, seeing that an heir apparent was not likely to live long under the existing circumstances, had sneaked Orestes out of Mycenae when her mother and Aegisthus, who had become Clytemnestra's lover, began to rule during the long absence of Agamemnon. In the manner of displaced and unwanted princes, he wound up in another king's court. As Orestes approached manhood in the court of King Strophius of Mount Parnassus, he learned what had happened back in Mycenae and faced a major problem. The great duty of a son was to avenge his father's murder. As Clytemnestra on the day of Agamemnon's death had come out of the palace covered in the king's blood and announced her vengeance, there was no doubt about the murderer's identity. Unfortunately, the greatest crime a child could commit was to kill a parent. Orestes could and would dispatch Aegisthus immediately, kinsman or no, but Clytemnestra was also guilty. Orestes went to the Delphic Oracle, which told him with unusual clarity to "shed blood for old blood shed" (Aeschylus *Choephori*.

chorus 4, strophe 2). He did as directed, and of course the Erinyes or Furies came after him. After much suffering, he was acquitted through the efforts of Apollo and Athena. He then went to reclaim Hermione, daughter of Menelaus and Helen, who had been promised to him in marriage but had been given to Neoptolemus/Pyrrhus, Achilles' son. Orestes slew Pyrrhus at the altar he had raised to Achilles and married Hermione.

But back to the story of Telemachus, son of Odysseus King of Ithaca. Almost ten years after the Trojan War Odysseus still had not come home, and his palace was full of loud (and greedy) nobles, warriors and hopefuls who were trying to persuade Penelope, Odysseus' queen, to marry them, as they were quite certain she was a widow by now. She deceived them for a long time by saying that she could not choose a husband until she had woven a shroud for her father-in-law Laertes. She wove during the day and unraveled by night, so that the shroud was never finished. Since even the densest of masculine stupidity has its limits, the suitors eventually grew suspicious.

The engraving shows the faithful Penelope outside at her loom. Penelope's cleverness is illustrated in the story of the shroud and again when she asks Odysseus to move their bed. Only the real Odysseus would know that their bed carved into an olive tree could not be moved.

The goddess Athena, having regained all her former partiality for Odysseus and wanting to help his family, had urged Telemachus to set out to find out what had happened to his father, and she had helped him to do so. In the court of King Nestor of Pylos, he received comfort and instructions to go on to King Menelaus in Sparta, who could fill him in on the fate of various Greeks. Menelaus told Telemachus about his own trials, the death of Agamemnon, and the fate of many other Greeks. Being a bit behind on the latest details, he also told Telemachus about Odysseus' captivity by the nymph Calypso on her island Ogygia.

Now that Odysseus was back, Athena hurried to Sparta and told Telemachus to go home, but she told him only that his grandfather and uncles were saying that Penelope should marry again. Menelaus gave him rich gifts, Athena gave him some good advice and good winds, and he soon returned home. With her usual craftiness, the goddess told Telemachus not to go to the palace, but to spend the night at the hut of the old faithful swineherd Eumaeus. A touching reunion followed, and then father and son sat down to plot together the undoing of the suitors.

As might be expected of any plan concocted by Odysseus, this one was good. Two men against all those suitors, even though some of them were abysmally stupid, could not be called great odds. So they agreed that Telemachus would go back to town alone, and while the suitors were enjoying Odysseus' wine, he would hide all their weapons. Odysseus, back in his withered beggar disguise, would follow with Eumaeus.

When they arrived for the daily feast, the suitors made fun of the poor old beggar, but Odysseus bore it patiently. Penelope, probably prompted by Athena, brought the great bow of Odysseus with its arrows from a storeroom and announced that she would marry the man who could bend it and shoot its arrow through twelve double-axes. Everyone tried, but no suitor could bend the thing. At last the old beggar asked to try it. The suitors cried out indignantly, but Telemachus insisted that the old man have his shot at it too. Odysseus shot the first arrow through the twelve axes and then turned the others on the suitors. They frantically reached for their weapons, which had been removed. After the arrows gave out, Odysseus, who had regained his great strength and skill along with his fine manly appearance, with the enthusiastic help of Telemachus finished off the rest of the suitors with spears. Needless to say there was a great feast of rejoicing in Ithaca that night.

Odysseus ruled for many years after his return. Tiresias (*Odyssey* 11.134–36) had told him that "a gentle death will come to you from the sea, when you are old and your people prosperous." Some later reports say he was killed in battle by Telegonus, a son Circe had borne to him years before and who did not know Odysseus was his father.

V: STARTING OVER

AENEAS AND THE BEGINNING OF ROME

Special Note: As we learn Aeneas' story from the Latin epic the AENEID, this section will reference the Roman Gods and their Roman names. For a complete listing of the Roman gods, please consult pages 55–56.

When Prince Aeneas reached the deserted temple of Ceres, which was the rendezvous for escaping Trojans, he put down his crippled father and turned, only to find that his wife had been separated from him as they passed through the city. He left his father and son with the other refugees and raged back through the city seeking her until at last her ghost appeared and told him she was dead. Sadly he returned to the meeting place to find a motley multitude of displaced Trojans which looked to him, as a scion of the royal line, for such trifles as food, shelter, and directions for what the dickens they should do next. He sighed, shouldered his father, and led them off to the foothills of Mount Ida to regroup.

The regrouping included building a fleet of twenty ships, as the smoking ruins of Troy were now a major disaster area and faraway places had been indicated by the gods. The fleet building lasted until summer, which was the only time anybody with a brain really wanted to sail the Mediterranean anyway. With ships filled with refugees, little household gods, scant belongings, a few choice gifts for bribing (oops, greeting) kings and other bigwigs they might meet, and some of those various animals the ancients were always offering to the gods, they sailed west into the Mediterranean Sea, as they had been given rather hazy instructions that they should make a new home in the west.

The adventures of Jason and Odysseus, among others, made it clear that the islands and shores of this body of water held many incredible inhabitants whom nobody in his right senses would ever want to meet. In addition the Trojans had to avoid a great many hostile Greek cities while seeking their destined new homeland. At least they did not start out, as the Greeks did after the Trojan War, with the collective enmity of all the gods. Neptune in particular had been kindly disposed toward

Aeneas even back during the Trojan War, when he called Aeneas great-hearted and said that Aeneas always gave the gods their full due. This divine approval would spare him part at least of Odysseus' watery trials. Juno, though, hated all Trojans in general and Aeneas in particular, since he was the son of Venus, who had inspired Jupiter's frequent misbehaviors and who had been awarded that Golden Apple in the Judgment of Paris. Moreover, he was destined to found a city which would be the destruction of Carthage, one of her favorite sites. The **Fates** had declared Aeneas' destiny, and the gods could not prevent it, but Juno, who was not only ox-eyed but bull-headed, was determined to try.

After a disastrous visit to Thrace, which involved bushes which bled when disturbed, on Apollo's island of Delos they were instructed to go to the home of their ancestors. After trying Crete, which Anchises said had been the original home of King **Teucer**, and encountering a famine and sickness there, they were informed by both the Penates, the little household gods of Troy, and later by an angry Harpy named Celaeno, that they should be going to Italy, from which Dardanus, Teucer's son-in-law, had come. As Celaeno added that from hunger they would eat their tables along with their food, the overawed Trojans lost no time in setting sail.

Sailing quickly past Ithaca with a few curses for Odysseus they put in at Actium, where they enjoyed a rest before going on to Buthrotum. There they were overjoyed to find Helenus, the son of King Priam of Troy, ruling with Andromache the widow of Hector as his queen. Andromache explained that she had been the war prize of Achilles' awful son Pyrrhus or Neoptolemus, who had given her to Helenus, also taken as a slave, when Pyrrhus himself had decided to wed Hermione of Sparta. That had been his undoing, however, as Orestes slew him before the altar of Achilles much as Pyrrhus himself had slain the aged King Priam. Helenus and Andromache had been able to retain this territory in Epirus, which was a remote area on the edge of Greece.

Helenus and Andromache welcomed the Trojans and heaped gifts upon them, and showed them the city they had built—a dollhouse Troy. There was a little Pergamum citadel, a miniature Scaean Gate, a little brook which they had christened Xanthus or Scamander after the roaring Trojan river that had done its best to drown all the Greeks. Aeneas and the Trojans appreciated the welcome and plopped their weary bodies down

AENEAS' JOURNEY
IN SEARCH OF A NEW HOME

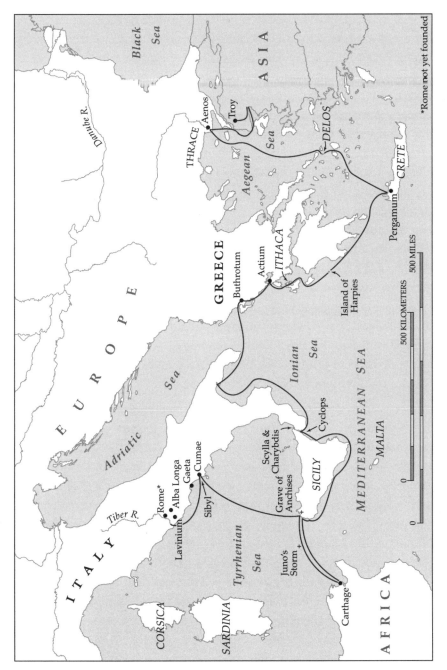

for a time. They refused all invitations to remain long, however. Aeneas had a duty, and he always honored such, and besides, looking backward is almost as deadening to progress as lotus eating. Helenus, who was a priest as well as a king, did in one of those long-suffering sacrificial bulls and delivered some very useful (and unusually specific) advice from Apollo. Aeneas was told to avoid the coast of Italy directly across from Greece, as it was held by some Greeks he did not want to meet, and to sail round to the west side of Italy instead. (Italy is basically a long, boot-shaped mountain range with a beach on each side, so going around it would be a much longer trip than going across it; however, given the unsavory types who sometimes inhabited it, going around could be worth the trouble.) Helenus also told Aeneas not to worry about having to eat the tables (this ingestion of dining furniture had been bothering the Trojans). He said Apollo would take care of that nasty-tempered (and nasty-smelling) Harpy's prediction. The big danger was that they would never get to Italy in one piece to eat furniture or anything else. Aeneas was strongly advised to keep sailing all around the island of Sicily, thus avoiding Scylla and Charybdis (whose perils Odysseus had previously encountered), and land in a great bay in western Italy. Then he was to seek an interview with the Cumaean Sybil, perhaps the most powerful of all Apollo's priestesses. And while carrying out all of Helenus' various instructions he was to make offerings to Juno at every opportunity. (Not that this was likely to help much, but there was no harm in trying.)

Aeneas and company sailed to Sicily, carefully following instructions, but Helenus had warned Aeneas that Juno was interfering somewhat with his priestly vision. Perhaps this was the reason that he mentioned neither the volcano Aetna, near which the Trojans spent a well-illuminated but uncomfortable night, nor the Cyclopes who inhabited that part of the island. Next morning the Trojans had hardly risen from their rest (using the term loosely) when they were accosted by a pitiful wreck of a man. The stranger stared at their Trojan clothing, hestitated, and then stumbled down to them. He cried that he was one of Odysseus' soldiers, and he had fought to destroy Troy, but that he would prefer to be killed by them in any manner they chose rather than to be lunch for Polyphemus or one of his brother Cyclopes. That insatiable Trojan curiosity which experience with Sinon had done nothing to discourage rose again. They asked him who he was, what was his family tree, and what had put him in such a deplorable state. He explained that he had signed on for the Trojan War because he lived in poverty in Greece, and he was now wishing he was back in that poverty. It seems that Odysseus, leaving the Cyclopes' isle in understandable haste after blinding Polyphemus, had put out to sea without this poor wretch. He told them, in dramatic and ghastly prose, the whole story of Polyphemus' blinding. He advised them to lose no time in sailing away and begged them to kill him or take him along. Polyphemus appeared on the skyline about this time herding his sheep and groaning, and his brother Cyclopes who had not been blinded began to appear here and there. The Trojans decided to heed the advice of the Greek. Taking him along, they sped back to the ships and hoisted sail with great dispatch.

Sailing around to the other side of the island, they found the city of King Acestes, who was of Trojan descent. Near his city Anchises died. Aeneas left his father's ashes with Acestes and set out to Italy to consult the Cumaean Sibyl, but divine double dealing intervened.

The goddess Juno had watched their adventures with a jaundiced eye, waiting for her chance to put them (both adventures and Trojans) to a summary end. She bribed Aeolus, King of the Winds, with her loveliest nymph to stir up a stupendous storm. The next thing the Trojans knew, everything went black, the waves were rising to the sky (or where the sky would probably be if one could still see it), and topsy and turvy were badly scrambled. Aeneas, grabbing a rope and feeling less than heroic at the moment, briefly envied the men who had died at Troy and then hung on and watched events. Of course, with the waves rolling to heaven and opening to expose the bottom of the sea [according to Vergil (Aeneid 1.106–7), who is fond of hyperbole], the sailors could barely hang on. All the ships were faring badly, but that of Orontes, leader of the Lycians, had the worst of it as it was sucked into a whirlpool and smashed into little pieces.

Neptune, his breakfast interrupted by all the noise, poked his head above the surface of the sea and took instant exception to all these happenings. He surmised that he owed this mess to his charming sister Juno, but he dealt first with the obvious culprits. Calling the winds to him, he made a few uncomplimentary remarks about their ancestry and probable ends. He ordered them to get back to their mountain and inform

Neptune astride his chariot rides the waves of a fountain at the royal palace in Versailles, France.

Aeolus that he would be along directly to discuss spheres of influence with him. Since Aeolus was only a minor god and Neptune was definitely one of the major ones, this message was unlikely to add much to Aeolus' comfort. Neptune then turned his attention (and his trident) to prying a few ships, which were festooning the rocks like displays at a fair, off their perches. The clouds, waters, and other miscellaneous ecological features thought well of putting their best foot forward as Neptune's chariot rolled majestically across the suddenly smooth waves.

Aeneas' people, those in the seven ships that were still in evidence, that is, looked around for land. They limped into a snug harbor resting between two great crags, where a rising forest and fresh water gushing from a cave promised rest. The Trojans plopped down on the shore, scraped the salt off their weary bodies, and set about drying their provisions and themselves after the recent sea bath. Meanwhile Aeneas, who was thirteen ships short, climbed a nearby rock to scan the sea, but saw no ships. He did, however, on turning his gaze back to land, see a flock of deer, so he supplemented the salty rations with some fresh venison. Back at camp he poured out wine (thoughtfully provided by King Acestes back in Sicily) all round and gave a bracing speech (he was feeling rather down in the mouth about the whole affair, but putting heart into the troops is part of a leader's job) while the meat was cooking. This speech helped the Trojans, but Aeneas was a number of friends short, and his optimism about the future sank to a low ebb.

Aeneas' mother Venus visited Jupiter while he was contemplating Juno's latest *fait accompli* to remind him of his promise that Aeneas would found a great race in Italy. As a result of her little visit Jupiter called Mercury away from whatever mischief he was up to (Mercury was god of both merchants and thieves, so he was probably up to a great deal) and ordered him down to Libya to the city of Carthage, which was close to the Trojans' landing spot. Mercury was to make its Phoenician inhabitants and their Queen Dido especially hospitable to any strangers who might show up.

Meanwhile back at the sea's edge Aeneas concealed his ships, and taking one friend, Achates, he set out on a "Tour of Exploration," keeping an eye peeled for dragons, hippogriffs, tiny people, giants, or other possibly unfriendly natives. What he saw was a lovely young thing dressed as a Spartan maiden going out to hunt game. (These comely young females were much given to hunting, sometimes for things other than the male of their species.) She was very chatty, telling him that he was in Libya and that the nearest city was Carthage, then favoring him with the tragic history of Dido, its beautiful young widowed queen. As she turned away he realized that she was his mother Venus. She paid no heed to his complaints about this role-playing habit of hers. She simply wrapped him and his friend in a mist, set them on the way to Carthage, and disappeared.

When they arrived in Carthage, Aeneas and Achates peered out from their cloud of mist and saw that Ilioneus the Trojan leader had arrived and was explaining to Queen Dido that he was in command of twelve ships that had survived the recent stormy blast. He needed repairs and news about Aeneas and the rest of the ships. She greeted him in that "Be Kind to Trojans" spirit bestowed by Mercury and offered to send scouting parties out looking for Aeneas.

Venus chose this opportune moment to dissolve the mist around Aeneas, first taking a moment to spruce him up with all the manly beauty she knew so well how to bestow. There followed greetings and explanations all round, and Dido sent food to all the ships, declared a holiday, and gave a sumptuous banquet. To the banquet Venus sent her mischievous son Cupid in place of little Ascanius/Iulus. As a result of this underhanded move, Dido fell madly in love with Aeneas and did her best to make him her new king and meld the two nations. Juno was all for this, but neither Venus nor, more importantly, the Fates, were having any part of this ploy to circumvent the founding of Rome.

The outcome of a love affair closely watched by this many deities with disparate agendas is unlikely to be happy. In Carthage Aeneas enjoyed a wonderful respite from his cares and all the joys a beautiful and besotted monarch could bestow on him. But Venus raged around Olympus, and Jupiter sent Mercury down to Aeneas, who was sporting a new cloak and a jeweled sword given him by Dido, with a very pointed message about duty. As Aeneas made preparations for departure, the nasty little demi goddess Fama informed Dido, who confronted Aeneas with a major soap opera scene. He told her that all he really wanted was to rebuild Troy with his bare hands, a sentiment that did very little to assuage her wrath. After another visit from Mercury, which warned him in no uncertain terms that it was now or never, Aeneas set sail, pausing only to host suitable funeral games for his father in Sicily before arriving at last in Italy. It was better for his peace of mind that he did not know how Dido spent the morning after she discovered his departure.

She dwelt with pleasure on some of the great old revenge methods; if only she had cut him in pieces and thrown him into the sea as Medea had done with Absyrtus, diced up little Ascanius/Iulus and served him to Aeneas in the manner of Atreus, or set the Trojan ships and camp afire and burned them all before she killed herself. Ah, well, such are the joys one has missed. Her only recourse at this late date was to pray for vengeance; in this she engaged with great zest. She called first upon the Sun, who sees all, then upon Juno, who no doubt listened with approval, then Hecate of the Witches, and last of all upon the Furies. Having called all these charming immortals who were in keeping with her mood to attention, she prayed that if Jupiter insisted on Aeneas' safe arrival in Italy and his founding of the promised city (which recent events indicated was a likely possibility) Aeneas should have no easy time of it while achieving his goal. For starters she asked that he should be beset by strong enemies in war, then driven from his homesteaded lands, and separated from Ascanius. The program of afflictions was then to include his begging for assistance, his witnessing the unmerited deaths of people he cherished, and his being forced to settle for an unjust peace. Her next gentle request was that after said unjust peace he should know no joy in his kingdom, but should die before his day and lie unburied in the sand. (Surely some of this nasty agenda came from the fertile mind of Juno; it was just her style.) Reversing a prayer she had made at the first banquet, she called upon the Carthaginians to hate all Aeneas' descendants, and to put that hate to good use with fire and sword. She prayed for unending general military turmoil and a special avenger to rise among her descendants. (Hannibal filled the bill nicely.) She rounded off the prayer with a request for shore to fight with shore and sea with sea (natural elements, like the birds, were often called upon to express sentiments hardly suitable to them), and with an earnest wish that every descendant of hers should be an enemy of every descendant of Aeneas'. Having outlined this pleasing program, she climbed upon a funeral pyre she had tricked her sister Anna into building and stabbed herself with that jeweled sword she had given Aeneas but which he had "thoughtfully" left behind.

The Trojans landed as instructed at Cumae and consulted Apollo's Cumaean Sibyl, who led Aeneas on a tour of the Underworld, as he was required to go there to consult his dead father Anchises. Anchises explained the world of the dead to his son and prophesied concerning many of the great men who through the generations would be Romans, Aeneas' descendants.

On leaving Cumae the Trojans sailed north along the Italian coast, and Neptune, who was still kindly disposed toward them, wafted the Trojans on a fair breeze so swiftly past Circe's isle that they scarcely heard the roars, oinks, and other assorted noises of her unfortunate guests. The wind dropped as the dawn broke, and the Trojans found themselves facing a great forest and the mouth of a clay-yellow river eddying into the sea. This would turn out to be the Tiber, one day to roll beneath the towers of Rome. At the moment it was rolling beneath the towers of King Latinus and his tribe, sensibly called the Latins (or sometimes the Laurentines, after a laurel tree the king had dedicated to Apollo). "This is it," cried Aeneas (*Aeneid* 7.35–36).

Now some of the gods who were kindly disposed toward the Trojans (or who knew how totally useless it was to try to fight the Fates) had been doing a little spadework with Latinus and his people. Latinus had no son to succeed him, but he had one very marriageable daughter who was being courted by every ambitious young sprig in the country. Turnus the Rutulian was the most powerful of these suitors as well as the most handsome, and he had had little trouble winning the vote of Amata, Latinus' queen, in the son-in-law balloting. But all of a sudden weird heavenly omens began frisking about all over the place. A great swarm of bees descended on the aforementioned laurel tree and, according to Vergil, who was a horticulturist as well as a poet, the bees locked all their little feet together and created a formidable clump. The soothsayers began explaining that this meant a stranger with a unified body of men (hopefully not clinging to each other by the feet) were approaching to take over. Before they had finished their speeches (which tended to be long), King Latinus with his lovely daughter Lavinia came to light the altar fires. Lavinia's headdress, jeweled crown, and hair burst into flame. Evidently some of the priestly crowd pointed out that this was divine fire (the sort of thing that happened from time to time in ancient days), for although no one doused Lavinia with water she was unharmed, and, indeed, she did light up the place. The ever ready soothsayers explained that this meant that the girl would bring both glory and a ruinous war to her people.

While Latinus was deciding that he should wed his daughter to a (hopefully strong and handsome) foreigner, Aeneas and the Trojans were relaxing down by the sea and preparing a meal. They laid out on the grass hard wheat cakes and piled fruits (and perhaps some leftover sacrificial meat) on these cakes and chomped away. As they polished off the last crumbs of these proto pizzas, Iulus said, "Look, Dad, we ate tables and all" (*Aeneid* 7.116). Aeneas remembered that unsettling prophecy about devouring the dining furniture and decided this was indeed the new home. He quickly twined a garland round his head and invoked gods known and unknown (which was quite a collection). Jupiter signaled OKAY! by thundering three times in a clear sky. The Trojans decided that this called for another feast, with lots of wine this time.

Soon Aeneas and his choicest men made a formal visit to the city of Latinus, and all was going well when Juno, with the help of Allecto, one of the worst of the Furies, stirred up Turnus and his would-be mother-in-law Amata to cause all sorts of havoc. A long and chaotic war ensued, in which both Aeneas and Turnus found allies among the various peoples of Italy.

Among others Aeneas's enemies visited a Greek immigrant named Diomedes, one of our old acquaintances from the Trojan War. Diomedes, engaged in building himself a new town, heard them respectfully enough, but made it plain that he was through fighting Trojans. The victory over Troy, he opined, had been a **Pyrrhic** one (although he didn't use that analogy, since Pyrrhus would not be born for several hundred years). He told how the victorious Greek leaders had been foiled in their attempts to arrive home from Troy. They were at the moment scattered all over the Mediterranean in various uncomfortable positions (with the single exception of the Greek commander Agamemnon, who had returned speedily to his city Mycenae only to be finished off by his vengeful spouse as soon as he arrived home). He himself was fairly comfortable in Italy, but he had been denied return to his home city Argos and his lovely wife. Furthermore, his outlook on life was not improved by the corpses of his fellow soldiers flying around over his head in the guise of birds making mournful cries. True, back in Troy in a moment of battle rage he had wounded Venus' hand as she tried to help Aeneas, and he had known from that moment that he had little reason to expect a happy ending, but no one else who crossed Aeneas' path seemed to prosper either. He suggested that they take the rich gifts the Latins had brought to him to Aeneas, and lose no time in making friends with him. He added as an unsettling afterthought that he had fought Aeneas, and if Troy had had two more like him it would still be standing.

When the war started in earnest, the Italians began to see Diomedes' point. They discovered just what it meant to face the Trojan warrior known around the ancient world as second only to the fabled Hector. When sacrificing to the gods, dodging love-smitten queens, or seeking allies, Aeneas was an impressive but harassed leader. On the battlefield, however, he was something else again—something likely to make his friends thank the gods that he was on their side and his enemies think seriously about peace talks. With spear and sword Aeneas mowed down Italians like a hurried farmer getting in his crops before a rain. After a great deal of time, and nearly six books of the *Aeneid,* had been spent in see-saw warring, Turnus agreed to what Aeneas had for some time been suggesting—a one-on-one combat to end the war. After a good bit of divine interference and dirty work, the two finally met in combat. Aeneas' spear caught Turnus in the thigh, and the giant warrior, stretched on the ground, begged that his body be honored. For a man who had spent much of his life slaying other warriors, Aeneas was unusually reluctant to kill anyone unless some cruel deed had raised that battle fury of his. He rested his hand on his sword-hilt, perhaps weighing the possibility of letting Turnus live and trying to work out a compromise. Then the sun, either because Apollo disapproved of this shilly-shallying or because the Fates had already decided the ending, caught the gleaming golden shoulder strap Turnus wore—Prince Pallas' sword-strap, which Turnus had stripped from the young prince's body and was now wearing as a battle trophy. This evidence of gloating over the death of a youngster almost as dear to Aeneas as his own son was too much. His anger blazed, and he sank the sword in Turnus' chest and sent him down to Hades.

After the war, Aeneas married Lavinia, and evidently founded a city in her honor named Lavinium. They had a son Silvius who would be the ancestor of Romulus and Remus, founders of Rome.

As is true with so many of our heroes, the exact circumstances of Aeneas' death are uncertain. Some say that three years after the peace he drowned in the river Numicius and his body was not recovered. (This story fits nicely that nasty curse of Dido's about Aeneas' dying before his day and lying unburied in the sand.) The historian Livy says Aeneas lies buried beside the Numicius. One legend even says that Venus asked Jupiter to make Aeneas a god. It states after the Numicius washed away his mortal parts, his mother anointed him with nectar and ambrosia, and he was later worshipped as Jupiter Indiges (not indigent, but indigenous, or home-grown). Whatever the exact facts may be, he seems to have gone on to his reward, whatever it was, soon after wedding Lavinia and producing another heir. He left behind the blended Trojan/Latin race, soon to be known as the Romans, before they started their long journey through history, slipping and sliding toward world domination. Thus he was spared the endless whirlpools of politics that have turned so many war heroes into frustrated old men and made them bald and bitter, rather than dead, before their time. Had Dido considered that aspect of the matter, she might have vented her spite by wishing him a long life.

So began the superheroes of the western world. They often died young, but they live forever. Their myths enthralled and inspired generation after generation and new names are still being added to their ranks. They are strong and brave, they persist in the face of impossible odds, they protect those who lack their talents, and they enshrine themselves in our memories as worthy mentors.

VI: SPECIAL NOTE

THE ROMAN GODS

The Romans often adapted the stories of the Greek gods to their own very similar deities. Both Zeus and Jupiter, for example, were sky gods and lords of the universe. As Greek Zeus the wide-ranging philanderer was more exciting than Roman Jupiter, who was a bit of a stuffed shirt, a little Roman borrowing is understandable. A general equivalency chart is given below.

The Twelve Roman *Dii Consentes* were similar in many ways to the Twelve Greek Olympians. Both mythologies also had two additional gods who held very high status, and there is a bit of disparity as to which ones make up the Big Twelve.

TWELVE *DII CONSENTES*

1. **Jupiter** (Zeus) - son of Saturn who dethroned his father and took his place as Lord of Sky and Earth and Superintendent of the Universe; one of the Capitoline Triad, the most powerful group of Roman gods, which was worshipped on the Capitoline Hill

2. **Juno** (Hera) - the wife and sister of Jupiter; Queen of Sky and Earth and the protectress of marriage; one of the Capitoline Triad

3. **Neptune** (Poseidon) - brother of Jupiter; god of waters.

4. **Ceres** (Demeter) - sister of Jupiter; goddess of grain; not an Olympian; mother of the stolen spring goddess Proserpina (the Greek Persephone) or Libera; member of the Aventine Triad with the wine god Liber and Libera

5. **Minerva** (Athena) - daughter of Jupiter and Metis, or wisdom; virgin goddess of warriors, poetry, medicine, wisdom, commerce, and crafts; the inventor of music; third of the Capitoline Triad

6. **Vesta** (Hestia) - goddess of civilized fire, or the hearth; her temple in Rome held the sacred fire, guarded by the Vestal Virgins

7. **Phoebus Apollo** - the son of Jupiter and Leto (Latona) and twin brother of Diana; god of the sun, truth, music, and medicine. In addition to his oracle at Delphi, Apollo had various other sibyls, or prophetesses, among whom was the Sibyl of Cumae.

8. **Diana** (Artemis) - twin sister of Apollo, who later became a three-fold deity: the goddess of hunting (Diana), of witches (Hecate), and of the moon (Selene); with Virbius god of woodlands and Egeria the water nymph she formed a triad of deities.

9. **Venus** (Aphrodite) - goddess of love and beauty who sprang from the sea; in some tales, the daughter of Jupiter. Through Iulus, son of Aeneas, she was claimed as the ancestress of the Julian clan.

10. **Mars** (Ares) - son of Jupiter and Juno; the god of war and father of Romulus and Remus

11. **Mercury** (Hermes) - son of Jupiter and Maia; the god of speed, trade, and thieves, as well as messenger of the gods

12. **Vulcan** (Hephaestus) - son of Jupiter and Juno; god of volcanoes; blacksmith god; wife was Venus.

THE "OTHER TWO"

13. **Pluto or Hades** - an Olympian, but not one of the Dii Consentes; dreaded ruler of the lower world (the dead). His stolen bride was Proserpina.

14. **Liber** (Bacchus/Dionysus) - god of wine; member of the Aventine Triad with Ceres and Libera

VII. NOTES

ABSOLUTION the forgiveness or remission of sin, often through a sacrifice or act of penance

ATREID descendant of Atreus, most commonly referring to Agamemnon or Menelaus

CENTAUR a race of creatures half human and half horse. Like the satyrs, who were half human and half goat, they were heavy drinkers and given to violence when intoxicated. Exceptional, perhaps unique, among them was Chiron, who was intelligent, civilized, and kind. He tutored many heroes, among whom were Heracles, Jason, Theseus and Aeneas.

CRONUS leader and the youngest of the Titans, divine descendants of Gaia, the earth, and Ouranus, the sky. He overthrew his father and ruled until he was overthrown by his own sons, Zeus, Hades, and Poseidon. His wife and sister was Rhea, mother of the Olympians.

DARDANUS son of Zeus and Electra who immigrated to the area of Mount Ida in western Asia Minor. This area was ruled by King Teucer, who welcomed Dardanus and allowed him to marry Batea, Teucer's daughter. Their city was Dardania. Their grandson Tros gave the name Troad to the area, and their great-grandson Ilus founded the city Ilium, which was also called Troy.

DELPHIC ORACLE the most important oracle, or religious advisor and foreteller of the future, in the classical Greek world. It was sacred to Apollo, god of truth, and was therefore infallible. The *omphalos* stone at Delphi marked the center of the earth and the universe. Answers to questions were given by the Pythia, Apollo's priestess, often in the form of a riddle.

ELEUSINIAN MYSTERIES closely guarded secret sacred rites carried out at the shrine of Demeter the grain goddess and her daughter Persephone at Eleusis. Initiates to these mysteries could call upon these gods in peril and in dangerous undertakings.

ERINYES female demon-deities who had snakes for hair and eyes that wept tears of blood. They were sent to punish the guilty, especially those guilty of murdering a relative. Chthonic deities motivated by bloodlust, they are also known as the Furies.

FATES usually called the Parcae in Latin, these three dreary females are said by the poets to have more power than any or all of the gods. Between them they create the web of life, with Clotho spinning the thread, Lachesis weaving the web, and Atropos cutting the thread at the end. What they have woven no god can change, as even Hera eventually found out.

HARPIES bird-like monsters with women's heads inhabiting the Strophades islands.

HUBRIS an overweening arrogance concerning one's own outstanding qualities combined with the incredible stupidity required to challenge the gods with those qualities. *Hubris* is a key concept in Greek tragedy.

KLEOS glory, fame, or the poem or song that reports the glory and fame; the medium and the message of heroic glory.

PERSEID descendant of Perseus

PYRRHIC VICTORY Pyrrhus was the King of Epirus who first fought the Romans in 280 BCE in southern Italy. He won, but lost so many soldiers that he said, "Another such victory will ruin me." Thus a Pyrrhic victory costs more than it is worth.

SEER one who could see things hidden, having the ability to predict the future or to speak for the gods.

TEUCER son of the river god Scamander and the nymph Idaea; king of the land around Mount Ida in western Asia Minor. The land was called Teucria for him, and later Dardania for his son-in-law Dardanus, who became king.

TRIBUTE money or goods paid, often to an enemy conqueror

TYRANNOS Greek term for absolute ruler, often one who usurped power.

BIBLIOGRAPHY

Burgess, J.S. *The Tradition of the Trojan War in Homer and the Epic Cycle.* Baltimore: John Hopkins University Press, 2001.

Colakis, Marianthe and Mary Joan Masello. *Classical Mythology and More: A Reader Workbook.* Mundelein, Illinois: Bolchazy-Carducci Publishers, 2007.

Curtius, Ernst Robert. *European Literature and the Latin Middle Ages.* London: Routledge and Kegal Paul, 1979.

Erskine, Andrew. *Troy Between Greece and Rome.* Oxford: Oxford University Press, 2003.

Ferguson, Diana. *Greek Myths and Legends.* New York: Collins and Brown, 2000.

Graves, Robert. *The Greek Myths.* London: Penguin Books, 1996.

Harris, Stephen L. and Platzner, Gloria. *Classical Mythology: Images and Insights.* New York: McGraw-Hill, 2003.

Hunt, J. William. *Forms of Glory: Structure and Sense in Vergil's Aeneid.* Carbondale, Illinois: Southern Illinois University Press, 1973.

Kerenyi, Karl. *The Heroes of the Greeks.* New York/London: Thames and Hudson, 1959.

Kirkwood, G.M. *A Short Guide to Classical Mythology.* Mundelein, Illinois: Bolchazy-Carducci Publishers, 2003.

Morford, Mark and Lenardon, Robert. *Classical Mythology.* 7th Edition. Oxford: Oxford University Press, 2002.

Newman, J.K. *The Classical Epic Tradition.* Madison, Wisconsin: University of Wisconsin Press, 2003.

Pinsent, John. *Greek Mythology.* New York: Peter Bedrick Books, 1982.

Putnam, Michael C.J. *Vergil's Aeneid: Interpretation and Influence.* Chapel Hill, North Carolina: University of North Carolina Press, 1995.

Rose, H.J. *A Handbook of Greek Mythology*. New York: Penguin Books, 1991.

Rouse, W.H. D. *Gods, Heroes and Men of Ancient Greece*. New York: New American Library, 2001.

Strauss, Barry. *The Trojan War: A New History*. New York: Simon & Schuster, 2006

Williams, Rose. *Gods and Other Odd Creatures*. Austin, Texas: Cicada-Sun Publishers, 2007

———. *The Labors of Aeneas*. Mundelein, Illinois: Bolchazy-Carducci Publishers, 2003.

———. *The Original Dysfunctional Family: Basic Classical Mythology for the New Millennium*. Mundelein, Illinois: Bolchazy-Carducci Publishers, 2008.

ANCIENT SOURCES

Aeschylus. *Oresteia.*

Apollodorus. *Bibliotheke* (*The Library*).

Apollonius of Rhodes. *Argonautica.*

Catullus. *Poem 64.*

Diodorus Siculus. *Bibliotheca Historica* (*Historical Library*).

Epic Cycle of Ancient Greek Poems.

Euripides. Plays.

Hesiod. *Theogony; Works and Days.*

Homer. *Iliad; Odyssey.*

Ovid. *Metamorphoses* (*Transformations*); *Heroides* (*The Heroines*).

Pausanias. *Description of Greece.*

Pindar. *Odes.*

Sophocles. Plays.

Statius. *Achilleis.*

Valerius Flaccus. *Argonautica.*

Vergil. *Aeneis* (*Aeneid*).

(For Latin texts, both the Latin title and its English translation are provided).

PHOTOGRAPHY CREDITS

LATIN FOR THE NEW MILLENNIUM ANCILLARIES

If you liked *The Clay-footed SuperHeroes*, you're sure to like these other fascinating works also written by Rose Williams

THE ORIGINAL DYSFUNCTIONAL FAMILY
BASIC CLASSICAL MYTHOLOGY FOR THE NEW MILLENNIUM

x + 62 pp (2008) 6" x 9" Paperback, ISBN 978-0-86516-690-5

A very accessible introduction to classical mythology, *The Original Dysfunctional Family: Basic Classical Mythology for the New Millennium* presents the key stories of the twelve Olympians as well as those of the two gods associated with the fruits of the harvest, Demeter and Dionysus. The Greek version of each Olympian is presented first followed by the Roman adaptation. Chock-full of information, this book provides a sound foundation for the beginning student's further studies in culture, literature, and history. The general reader will find Williams' style engaging.

Features:

- Greek version of each Olympian followed by the Roman adaptation
- Genealogical charts of the Olympian family and their offspring
- Each set of stories presented in chronological order
- Notes section for Latin and other special terms employed in the text
- Illustrations drawn from the corpus of ancient sculpture

LATIN FOR THE NEW MILLENNIUM
ANCILLARIES

If you liked *The Clay-footed SuperHeroes,* you're sure to like these other fascinating works also written by Rose Williams.

FROM ROMULUS TO ROMULUS AUGUSTULUS
ROMAN HISTORY FOR THE NEW MILLENNIUM

(2009) 6" x 9" Paperback, ISBN 978-0-86516-691-2

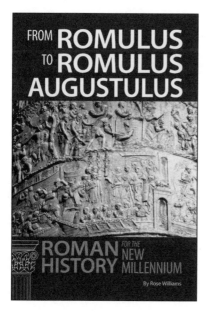

Readers will delight in the fascinating stories of Rome—the quirky, the gory, and the momentous. This book will serve as the perfect companion for the student beginning to study Latin or as an accessible introduction to Roman history for the general reader. Recognizing the symbiotic relationship between literature and the period in which it was produced, *From Romulus to Romulus Augustulus: Roman History for the New Millennium* provides a comprehensive overview of Roman history and Latin literature.

Features:

- Assessment of the critical events in Roman history
- Presentation of the key historical and literary figures of Rome
- Timeline of Roman history from its foundation to Theodoric
- Notes section for Latin and other special terms employed in the text
- Authentic illustrations from the Roman era

LATIN FOR THE NEW MILLENNIUM ANCILLARIES

If you liked *The Clay-footed SuperHeroes*, you're sure to like these other fascinating works also written by Rose Williams

FROM ROME TO REFORMATION
EARLY EUROPEAN HISTORY FOR THE NEW MILLENNIUM

(2009) 6" x 9" Paperback, ISBN: 978-0-86516-718-6

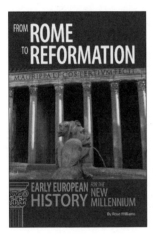

Rose Williams skillfully leads the reader through the maze of power plays and the gradual rise of sovereign states that followed the collapse of the Roman Empire. Readers will appreciate Williams' engaging style and her ability to synthesize succinctly this busy period of history. Recognizing the symbiotic relationship between literature and the era in which it was produced, *From Rome to Reformation: Early European History for the New Millennium* provides a comprehensive overview of the interconnecting historical events, literary figures, and intellectual developments in European history and its Latin literature. This is a perfect companion text for courses in the humanities, western civilization, and Latin.

Features:

- Overview of the history of ideas developed in western civilization
- Assessment of the critical events in early European history
- Presentation of the key historical and literary figures of early Europe
- Timeline of European history from the fifth century to the eighteenth
- Notes section for Latin and other special terms employed in the text
- Illustrations enhance the text

FOLLOW YOUR FATES

Follow Your Fates is a series of books that allows the reader to participate in the story by making choices that affect the course of the narrative. The reader assumes the role of the hero-protagonist and makes choices that determine the hero's responses to the unfolding plot.

After a brief introduction to the story, the reader is placed in the middle of the action and at crucial points is asked to choose between two or more next courses of action. In the series' first book, *The Wrath of Achilles*, the reader assumes the role of Achilles, the greatest hero of ancient Greece, and confronts the same dilemmas Achilles faced in Homer's *Iliad*. The plot branches out and unfolds to decision after decision, leading to multiple possible endings. Should Achilles stay true to his honor code and not fight, or stand beside his countrymen and win even more fame and glory, but seal his own death? The reader must decide.

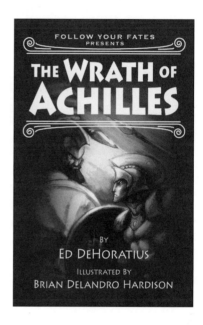

Follow Your Fates is patterned after a popular gamebook style and is designed for fans of the classics. In addition to *The Wrath of Achilles*, the series will include:

The Journey of Odysseus

The Exile of Aeneas

In Ed DeHoratius' gripping stories, each dynamically illustrated by award-winning comic book artist Brian Delandro Hardison, readers ages eight and up can experience firsthand the choices fate handed three epic heroes of ancient Greece and Rome. What better introduction to classic literature?

WHEN IN ROME
BEST CARTOONS OF POMPEIIANA NEWSLETTER

Edited by Marie Carducci Bolchazy

viii + 80 pp (2009) Paperback 978-0-86516-717-9

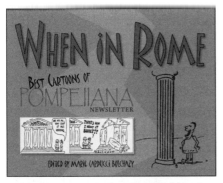

Every Latin student should have a copy of this book. Test how savvy you are about myth and Roman history. Who knew the ancient world could be so funny? This collection of cartoons was taken from the archives covering 26 years of publication of *Pompeiiana*, a newsletter devoted to student-developed material. Popular topics for the cartoons include Medusa (e.g., her chicken-haired cousin), Julius Caesar (e.g., Caesar reforms the colander), the Trojan War (e.g., Ulysses getting a Trojan warrior to shout his comments thus making the Trojan hoarse) as well as commentary on Caligula's horse in the senate (always voting "neigh") and Horatius playing cards or Horatius at bridge.

Features

- 138 cartoons taken from the archives of *Pompeiiana*, a newsletter for students of Latin
- Original artwork
- Special sections on Medusa cartoons
- Foreword by Dr. Bernard Barcio, editor of the *Pompeiiana* for 26 years
- Forthcoming companion book, using more material from the *Pompeiiana* archives

About the Editor

Marie Carducci Bolchazy has a doctoral degree in education from the State University of New York at Albany and a master's degree, also in education from Cornell Unversity. She currently works full-time at Bolchazy-Carducci Publishers, which she co-owns with her husband. One of their specialties is Latin books. She has always admired the *Pompeiiana Newsletter* and thoroughly enjoyed selecting her favorite cartoons from its archives.

HOW THE GRINCH STOLE CHRISTMAS, LATIN EDITION

(*originally published in English by Random House, New York: Random House, 1957.)

QUOMODO INVIDIOSULUS NOMINE GRINCHUS CHRISTI NATALEM ABROGAVERIT

Dr. Seuss; Original Dr. Seuss illustrations
Translator: Jennifer Morrish Tunberg with Terence O. Tunberg

64 pp (1998)
    Paperback: 8 x 11 ISBN 978-0-86516-420-8
    Hardbound: 8 ¼ x 11 ¼ ISBN: 978-0-86516-419-2

Every Latin student should have a this wonderful story in Latin in their library! The timeless tale of how the true spirit of Christmas captured the heart of the irascible Grinch is retold in Latin in *Quomodo Invidiosulus nomine GRINCHUS Christi natalem Abrogaverit*. This edition features the original artwork of Dr. Seuss and a translation that echoes the word play and rhythmic narrative of the world's best-selling children's author.

The wonderful, whimsical and thought-provoking stories of Dr. Seuss have been published in twenty languages. An excellent addition to Seuss collections the world over, this Latin-language edition of Seuss' timeless Christmas classic is a welcome, all-occasion gift, a delightful way to revisit a treasured tale, and an enjoyable way to refresh your high school Latin.

Features:

- excellent Latin translation that echoes the word play and rhythmic narrative of the original
- original artwork of Dr. Seuss
- Latin-to-English vocabulary
- note on the translation

GREEN EGGS AND HAM* IN LATIN
VIRENT OVA! VIRET PERNA!!

Dr. Seuss

Translated By Jennifer Morrish Tunberg and Terence O. Tunberg

72 pp., Original Dr. Seuss illustrations throughout (July 2003)

6 1/2" x 9" Hardbound, ISBN 978-0-86516-555-7

Sam-I-am's smiling enthusiasm for the seemingly unappetizingly tinted green eggs and ham is undaunted, despite repeated disdain shown by an unnamed, dour disparager. Sam will not give up, though, and offers the dish over and over, proposing that it be sampled under sometimes whacky circumstances and in odd locales (with a goat, on a boat, in the rain, on a train, in a box, with a fox, etc.). In the end Sam does get the grumpy disparager to take a taste—if only to get Sam off his back. The disparager's demeanor quickly changes to all smiles when he discovers to his surprise that disdained green eggs and ham are, in fact, quite tasty. Sam-I-Am, yet another delightfully plucky Seuss protagonist, allows both adults and humans to look—with the objectivity humor so adeptly affords—at our all-too-human tendency towards knee-jerk negativity in response to anything that is new or different.

Dr. Seuss' perennial favorite, *Green Eggs and Ham*, is here rendered in spirited Latin: in trochaic rhythm with rhyme in the last two syllables, a sprightly verse-form that goes toe-to-toe with Seuss's whimsical drawings. *Virent Ova! Viret Perna!!* is a true delight—Latin as it is infrequently experienced: fun, exhilarating, ebullient. This Latin-language edition is a welcome, all-occasion gift, a delightful way to revisit a treasured tale, and an enjoyable way to refresh your high school Latin. It features

- Fast-moving Latin translation that echoes the lighthearted spirit of the original
- Original artwork of Dr. Seuss
- Latin-to-English vocabulary
- Note on "How to Read these Verses"